the
MAGIC
of
NATURE

© Katherine M. Blanner

About the Author

Jessica's motto is "adventure first, then write!" When not running around exploring nature, she chases after multiple versions of herself and looks after animal babies. She has also written *Walk Your Path*, *The Golden Rule*, *My Family Is Different*, and many more titles. Her writing has won two Missouri Writer's Guild Awards among countless others. She is a columnist for *Witch Way Magazine*, a member of SCBWI, and a fan of chasing butterflies. As a dyslexic Pagan, Jess loves all types of people but has a soft spot for differing minds.

Publications that have featured Jessica Marie Baumgartner's work include *Magic of Motivational Poetry and Quotes*, *Evie Magazine*, *Father and I*, *Woods Reader*, *Light of Consciousness Magazine*, *Breastfeeding Today*, *Conscious Shift Magazine*, *New Spirit Journal*, *LitReactor*, *Buddy Lit Zine*, *The St. Louis Post Dispatch*, *Kid's Imagination Train*, *Mothers Always Write*, *RAC Magazine*, *My Wandering Uterus*, *Guardian Angel Kids* ezine, *FrostFire Worlds*, *Chicken Soup for the Soul: Inspiration for Teachers*, *Circle Magazine*, *The Witches' Voice*, *Spirit One* magazine, *Walrus Publishing*, and the *Saint Louis Examiner* (where she got her start as a Pagan columnist about a decade ago).

Jessica Marie
Baumgartner

the

MAGIC
of
NATURE

MEDITATIONS & SPELLS
TO FIND YOUR
INNER VOICE

LLEWELLYN PUBLICATIONS
WOODBURY, MINNESOTA

FIRST EDITION
First Printing, 2021

Book design by Samantha Peterson
Cover design by Shira Atakpu
Editing by Laura Kurtz

Llewellyn Publications is a registered trademark of Llewellyn Worldwide Ltd.

Library of Congress Cataloging-in-Publication Data
Names: Baumgartner, Jessica Marie, author.
Title: The magic of nature : meditations & spells to find your inner voice
   / Jessica Marie Baumgartner.
Description: First edition. | Woodbury, Minnesota : Llewellyn Worldwide,
   Ltd, 2021. | Summary: "Mostly solitary nature-based magic practices for
   the experienced outdoors enthusiast"— Provided by publisher.
Identifiers: LCCN 2020057920 (print) | LCCN 2020057921 (ebook) | ISBN
   9780738767857 (paperback) | ISBN 9780738768465 (ebook)
Subjects: LCSH: Nature—Miscellanea. | Magic.
Classification: LCC BF1623.N35 B38 2021 (print) | LCC BF1623.N35 (ebook)
   | DDC 158.1/28—dc23
LC record available at https://lccn.loc.gov/2020057920
LC ebook record available at https://lccn.loc.gov/2020057921

Llewellyn Worldwide Ltd. does not participate in, endorse, or have any authority or responsibility concerning private business transactions between our authors and the public.
   All mail addressed to the author is forwarded but the publisher cannot, unless specifically instructed by the author, give out an address or phone number.
   Any internet references contained in this work are current at publication time, but the publisher cannot guarantee that a specific location will continue to be maintained. Please refer to the publisher's website for links to authors' websites and other sources.

Llewellyn Publications
A Division of Llewellyn Worldwide Ltd.
2143 Wooddale Drive
Woodbury, MN 55125-2989
www.llewellyn.com

Printed in the United States of America

Other Books by Jessica Marie Baumgartner

Walk Your Path: A Magical Awakening (Green Magic Publishing, 2020)

The Golden Rule (Eleventh Hour Literary Press, 2017)

My Family Is Different (THG StarDragon Publishing, 2014)

To the wild spirit that lives in us all.

CONTENTS

INTRODUCTION

The world has changed drastically in a very short period. We have distanced ourselves from nature and lost our instinctual connection that leads to enlightenment. Our instincts have spoken to us for thousands of years. Generation upon generation relied on listening to the energies surrounding them and trusting in themselves. Those connections still exist—they lie dormant within us all. The inner voice that once warned of coming invaders, plagues, and devastation remains in hibernation for many, and it can be reawakened.

The human body is electric. It hosts more power than we will ever harness. We forget this fact; our parents forgot, too. It's time to remember our ancestors and to reconnect with healthy natural living. Nothing can ever truly stamp out the instinctual calling, but it's time to reactivate the natural instincts that guide our more spiritual selves.

A great shift is coming. Whether we desire change or not is irrelevant. Preparation is necessary if we wish to retain our rights and our lives. We deserve food, clean water, clear air, and above all, the ability to care for ourselves and our energies. Laughter, love, and liberty must not be forgotten.

A fire is brewing inside of me. The need to break free bubbles within until I feel as if it must be unleashed to guide a new phase into being. It is during these surges of insight that I find it necessary to unplug. My rule is to take at least one day away from technology each week; it lets the static fade and allows me to be the only person in my own head for a while. And it is these periods that bring certain questions to mind: How many Westerners know how to cook full course meals from scratch or grow their own food from seeds they harvested for future planting seasons? If lost in the woods, how many would be able to read a map, use a compass, or follow the stars or the sun to find their way out? Without matches, could they start a fire? If starving, could they hunt or fish, or identify which wild berries are safe to eat? Is it possible that people can still make their own clothes and survive harsh winters without electricity?

These are the questions that matter. Those with the skills to be self-sufficient hold the ability to protect others, preserve themselves and their loved ones, and harbor the power and energies to maintain or restore order and balance with dignity and poise.

My direct links to the natural world are what carried me through disaster and tragedy in my life. Learning to trust my inner voice and recognize a deeper calling has gifted me insight and self-control that lends perspective and the ability to face any situation when needing to help myself or others. There has not been a single time in my life where this did not lead me down a better path.

The method for developing this instinct is detailed in this book's chapters, in addition to options for times when one is unable to go out and explore (such as in-home planting or simple star gazing). Guidance is written to reincarnate the instincts and offer advantages to those willing to learn. These instincts lead to many benefits for individuals, their communities, countries, and the world itself. Whether a person wishes to lead a more fulfilling life, aid their neighbors and loved ones, or create a positive effect for future generations, it all starts with our instincts and how we apply them to modern life.

A person can get in tune with the ancient calling through meditation, ritual, and spellwork. All meditations have their place. Rituals work based on the individual making use of them. Like everything in life, spells can be perfected over time.

The explosive technological age has provided many unexplored paradoxes. Its flow of constant input has connected us more than ever but can also diminish our individual senses of self. The mindset for community-based efforts still lives in our blood. These instincts drive our compassion for others and even our misgivings to better help us navigate our surroundings. That said, the world has changed and we must change with it. In order to push out the noise and focus on what matters most, a person has to learn the art of stillness—simple, peaceful quiet.

There are times when it's best to let the world take us away, but the times to clear the mind and work on strengthening our brains are just as important. Meditation is the entryway to the spirit. It opens new pathways and leads to inner peace. It is the easiest way to reach out to instinct and seek answers buried within.

From simple breathing exercises to deeper guided explorations, meditation makes its practitioners self-aware and more perceptive. Life is a constant work in progress; meditation outlines the plot and places it at the forefront of our sight.

Getting away from the chaos that is our daily lives to meditate on what has existed before us is the first step. Granted, not everyone can just pack up and leave—if you wish to find a wooded area to escape traffic and listen to the birds, it is just a matter of taking a walk or opening a window. Stepping into the greater realm means connecting with an entire environment. If you are unable to walk, sitting among the elements is always possible.

The setting and timing for connecting to nature varies. Never trespass on private property or directly endanger yourself for this purpose. It is important to use common sense and take the proper precautions to abide by human decency as well as the law.

We must all listen to, absorb, use, and share our connections to meet the future fates as deserving creatures who have walked with this planet's other inhabitants. Every single being has a purpose. Nothing is wasted in nature. Are you ready to meet your fate?

1
EARTH MEDITATIONS

Trees, meadows, and caves hold more magic than anyone can harness. They host life and death with balance. Harsh rules and tender moments exist in countless instance. Breaking free from the pretentious expectations of societal strain provides the calming effects one needs to be at peace with themselves and find the answers they seek living captive within.

Tree meditations remind me of my own potential. Everything starts small. No matter what shape or size the seed, there is opportunity for growth if nurtured properly. Even when beset by storms, fires, or unnatural destruction, trees will bud, bloom, and regrow—sometimes from the center of their own decimated stumps.

Trees represent longevity. They mark the passing of eras and generations. Acknowledged or not, they shelter and nourish life, in doing so producing enough energy to aid anyone on a quest for purpose and accomplishment.

If mobility is an issue, the easy meditations provide the groundwork for more challenging mental explorations. Opening windows and procuring potted trees, grasses, and sand gardens allows connections to be cultivated without as much physical strain. After training your mind to work with the body and spirit to connect with the earth, you can extend and use visualization for further development.

EASY TREE MEDITATION

This practice is an exercise in patience and humility. It displays how small the human world truly is when separated from the bosom of the forces that birthed it. Best done without shoes on, this tree meditation cultivates a deeper relationship between instinct and consciousness.

The Easy Tree Meditation requires standing before a tree trunk.

1. Place hands against the bark.
2. Stare upward and focus on the network of leaves, limbs, branches, and twigs.
3. Feel the air pass through the lungs with each breath.
4. Allow the energies within the wood to mingle with skin. Notice any new thoughts that emerge.

SITTING TREE MEDITATION

For longer explorations, it is best to sit underneath a tree with your back against the trunk, preferably in between any aboveground roots. Instead of relying on your sense of sight, this meditation requires more trust, which will deliver a new perspective. For the Sitting Tree Meditation:

1. Close your eyes.
2. Press your hands on the ground on either side of you or let them rest on nearby roots.
3. Hum with the wind, or if none, let out a quiet tone.
4. Listen to the vibrations. Feel the energy of the tree, the life, the structure. Mingle the vibrations with that electricity. It may tingle.
5. Allow time to fall behind. Remain fixed to the space as if rooted until called back to earthly ties by either a vision or whisper, or until the tingling stops.

CLIMBING TREE MEDITATION

Those who can safely do so (having the agility, flexibility, endurance, and practice) can partake of meditations up in the boughs. There's a different atmosphere in the arms of our towering oxygen makers. Pulling yourself up limb by limb requires patience and trust. Extending trust to your own physical prowess and your ability to estimate the strength of a limb is like air for thought.

Instead of equations solved on paper, these puzzles exist in the physical world. Tangible solutions are more necessary—one wrong move and injury can occur.

Tree meditations first require the climb (or proper mental image of climbing), but that is the precursor. Once situated as high as comfort allows, the Climbing Tree Meditation begins:

1. Sit on a branch or branches strong enough to support your weight.

2. Slide your fingers over the bark.

3. Breath deep and imagine the roots digging as deep under the tree as the branches reach.

4. Think of their purpose, their continuous reaching for a sun they cannot touch.

5. Imagine life struggles and how they relate to personal goals and future plans.

6. Think of the growth, the journey. Imagine the brain as if each crease were a branch reaching for more knowledge. No one can learn everything, but to seek answers is part of the human condition. Let the questions dance with what answers have already been found.

7. A sense of peace and calming should conclude the meditation.

EASY FIELD MEDITATION

Children find happiness easily; they are more in tune with their instincts. They trust themselves more than anyone else and their wants and needs come first. Not to be mistaken with immaturity, the inner child is that part of ourselves that gets excited and loves deeply without fear. I still roll down hills and chase butterflies through fields because it connects me to my environment. Simply sitting in a field or meadow and soaking up the fresh air and sunshine holds the power to recharge the human body.

The Easy Field Meditation is enlightening and effortlessly done:

1. Find a spot to sit on the grass or dirt.

2. Rub palms over the ground around you.

3. Close your eyes and inhale.

4. Open your eyes and look to the sky. Exhale.

5. Once more, close your eyes and breathe in.

6. With each breath, feel the rhythm of the ecosystem. Hear the animals. Smell the air.

7. With each exhale, glance at the habitat and appreciate it for what it is.

8. Think of how people fit in to what you are seeing. What can they do to better complete the areas they inhabit? Focus on the births and deaths that must take place to allow life to continue its purpose—find peace in your contemplation.

Wind Meditations

Change crescendos in the wind. It glides over and through the world without being seen but leaves behind ample evidence of its power. Each season experiences its gusts and gales. Whether harsh or gentle, each aspect of this powerful element holds connections to our primal needs, inspiring or setting us on the path to create our own whirlwinds even if we cannot venture far from our porches or doorways.

WINTER WIND MEDITATION

Outdoor meditation during the harshest weather requires sacrifice that is well worth the discomfort. As we age, the shock of winter's cold runs deeper and deeper. Aches and pains surface that had never previously made themselves known.

The thought of venturing outside to immerse the mind in nature during this time may seem too uncomfortable to attempt, but it is necessary for healing relief.

It's recommended that you have a warm drink and blankets in a comfortable spot waiting for you after this meditation. Before that comes the rush, numbness, and strengthening of the Winter Wind Meditation:

1. Find a space to sit on the hard ground, or even in snow on a windy day.

2. Acknowledge every single bodily ailment. Feel the pain and think of it as a glowing red light.

3. Close your eyes and feel the wind. Smell how it cleanses. Hear it whip through. Taste the slight peppermint, but mostly feel the harsh switch in temperature.

4. Visualize that each gust holds a light. White or blue.

5. Let that light wash over the red aches and pains. Let it overpower the hurt of flesh.

6. Gently stretch the head and neck, followed by the wrists, arms, ankles, and legs.

7. Roll up into a standing position and let the wind empower the spine. Use its energy for the benefit of the body.

8. Look to the sky and bow.

9. Go inside and get warmed back up. There should be a great sense of relief.

SPRING BREEZE MEDITATION

With a new season comes new opportunities. Spring is a time for hope, rebirth, renewal, and increasing personal energies. There is always something new coming or going. Splotches of color paint dry, dead landscapes to call the wild back to its vibrant self.

In nature, destruction has purpose—to break down the weak and make way for what is stronger, newer.

In contrast is the relationship between humanity and the cycles that exist around us. Instead of fighting the inevitable, embracing it and preparing ourselves gives us the strength of mind that can lead to our stronger selves.

A simple Spring Breeze Meditation is all one needs to find a place in this chaos:

1. Sit near a garden on a windy day.

2. Listen to the air's cries—are they sad or happy? Do they hold a message?

3. Sway in time with each blow.

4. Extend your mind to the wavering airways.

5. Follow the gusts. Where are they going? Where did they come from? Are they growing, dying, or showing off?

6. Think of life in relation to these questions.

7. Let the wind blow each thought in the right direction. Where are you going? Where did you come from? Is there still room for growth, death, and sharing talents?

8. Take the answers. Stand and finish, walking with a purpose.

SUMMER GALE MEDITATION

Life abounds in summer. New creatures are old enough to explore life. The elderly get a second wind, and the season's warmth forces everyone to replenish their own resources with fresh liquids. Like the extreme temperatures of winter, summer's heat draws deeper thoughts.

The purpose of the Summer Gale Meditation is to push away the unwanted and detrimental energies, habits, connections, and ailments from the self:

1. Find a field full of long grasses or wildflowers on a windy day—the higher they reach, the better.

2. Walk into the center of the field. With each step, brush your fingertips over tops of the growth. Let the plants graze your palms.

3. Once centered, rest your hands among the heads of the vegetation. The winds will move them over still skin. Look to the sky.

4. Now close your eyes. Each movement is a change. No matter how minuscule, it matters to the simple lives it touches. Use that energy to focus on the swish and sway of the grasses and/or flowers.

5. Imagine yourself as one of these plants. Rooted in your past, think of the earliest memories as the sprouting of a seed. Follow those memories through the stages of life that have flowered, withered, and returned once more in new colors, like changing perennials.

6. Now think of the parasites and pests that have caused harm. How they have built a stronger stalk and deeper roots. Think of them not

as evil or great wrongs that caused pain but flecks of decay that simply needed to break down in the stirring wind.

7. With each new gale, the energy will build. When all stages have been recalled, turn back to the present. Open your eyes. See the effects of a great invisible force bending masses of plant life to its will. Smile at it. Embrace it.

8. Ask the wind to help blow away what is currently stunting new growth. Focus on change and letting go. Know that the wind alone cannot guide a person but is beside everyone at all times.

9. When all seems clear, raise your arms to the sky. Spin in a circle clockwise, then counterclockwise. Bow.

AUTUMNAL GUST MEDITATION

Autumn is a perfect time to stop and appreciate all that life holds. To obtain the right mindset and survive the sleepy winter without depression or claustrophobia, humans need respite from summer's extremes. The gusts that flit about are more welcome as we embrace familiar traditions. In honor of nearing the end of the year, this exercise is about appreciating the here and now, the moments where we always find ourselves no matter how we feel.

1. Step outside on a windy day. No matter what kind of structure you live in—studio apartment, condo, townhouse, cottage, house, or mansion—go to the front door.

2. Stand outside the door as if you are a guest about to knock. Focus on the gusts rushing around you. Block out all else—do not allow yourself to feel silly.

3. Rest your hands on the door and lean against them. Think of what home means—how it protects, secures, and enhances life.

4. Imagine life without a home of any kind. The freedom may be nice or offer some benefits, but it does not give consistency or stability. The wild world may not have written laws, hired patrols, or elected officials and judges; it is built upon a set of rules older than any human. The winds would not be as forgiving. Recognize that and focus on all your

living space has given you. No matter how small, cramped, or worn down, it is there and is a part of life.

5. Feel the energies inside your chest reaching for that home as each chilly breath of nature warns the skin of coming harshness. Internally thank yourself for having met basic needs. No matter how humble, celebrate any source of shelter, clothing, and food.

6. Bow your head and close your eyes. Think of whether this home is the best place for your situation. If it suits you, thank it as well, slowly and wholeheartedly. If it is a burden or a temporary waiting place, thank it for the time being and also visualize the kind of space that awaits—something more suited to your personality, lifestyle, and tastes. Imagine how to obtain that new space. Do not fear work or failure. Just focus on how to get there.

7. Knock on your door and open it. Look around and smile at what you currently have. Appreciate it. No matter what is lacking, there is always someone or something mingling with your spirit.

Bonfire/Campfire Meditations

Fire may as well be a living being. It is born as if from nowhere. It eats, sleeps, can reawaken, and die. And despite its lack of both sentience and a continuous structure, it is a powerful element for survival. It is also a magical tool.

Humanity's use of fire as a source of power, light, and heat dates back before recorded history. It is so closely linked to survival and culture that it still holds significance in our lives. This great element mystifies. It changes the atmosphere of any setting. Within the heart of the flames and each glowing ember is great energy. Fire lends strength to the freezing. It offers crackling laughter for the lonely. It burns the foolish and mars the weak.

For individuals like myself it is a gateway. When sitting before glowing heat waves, I am inspired to indulge in complexity of thought and drift through storytelling or scrying. At the right times it provides the proper guidance for rituals and spells as well as prayer and fasting.

Setting a circle of stones or digging a pit requires nothing more than a little elbow grease. When outside aid is required, a trusted friend or family member can be called on to help build a fire.

Common sense should tell a person to keep away from trees, shrubs, and plants that easily catch fire. The gathering of dry wood and dead grasses for kindling is an offering that builds a deeper connection. Collecting sticks, twigs, and fallen branches is its own meditative process, but the sense of accomplishment that comes from starting one's own fire is just the start of the powers that build from this exercise in self-reliance. It leads to confidence, trust, and self-awareness.

It takes practice to fully explore these meditations. At first they may feel silly or uncomfortable, but those feelings come from a lack of confidence, faith, or direction. Fire has shared many triumphs and tragedies with humanity. It is a relation, a friend. Treat it as such, but be careful with it.

SMALL FIRE MEDITATION

When inexperienced, it is often best to start small. It is also advised that people with great experience humble themselves and revisit smaller scale practices to elevate their pattern of growth.

The fires of our ancestors burn within our very bodies now. The answers, meditations, and prayers never die. A Small Fire Meditation calls to them. It opens the soul's eyes just enough to provide an ample amount of personal power but nothing so drastic as to overwhelm, mislead, or corrupt. When finished, enjoy the fire. There is no rush to put it out and move on to a new task.

1. Build and light a small fire. (Never use lighter fluid or other potent chemical fuels. It is best to light with flint rocks, a magnifying glass, or matches. Use a lighter as a last resort.)

2. Sit before the flames. Stare into the jetting heat. Move close enough to feel the warmth.

3. Breathe in the cleansing smoke. Let it wash over the body. Sit tall with good posture.

4. Clear the mind. Listen to the slight hiss and fizzle.

5. Look to the center of the flames. Allow your vision to defocus, but keep your mind sharp; do not let your thoughts wander. Feel the power of your brain sync with the movements of the fire in front of you.

6. If you find it helpful, gently rock or sway your body. A sensation that feels like the mind is widening may occur—this is good. Will the fire to protect and guide but allow the rush of energy in your chest to meld with the throbbing impulse of your mind as if the two are one.

7. Give this meditation time. Do not fear failure. It may take many attempts but eventually the body will become ignited with energy as if part of the fire. Goose bumps or a tingling sensation may spread over the limbs. This is a shared energy that reconnects the modern person to the ancient call of the wild. When this energy is shared, it draws forth lost instincts that can be later worked into chants, prayers, or spells (two sides of the same coin).

CAMPFIRE MEDITATION

Campfires are stronger than small sparks but have no need to reach high into the sky like a great bonfire. These are the midrange flames that lick at firewood quickly while delivering a deeper range of heat. They also require more tending.

Instead of just sitting before the flames and losing myself, a deeper connection has to be forged. I connect best when I find a good long branch strong enough to withstand the fire in short bursts. It serves as a staff to control rogue twigs but is also itself a sacrifice that will eventually be set ablaze.

Build the fire as before, but place a few thicker sticks and shortened tree limbs that have fallen on their own. Let the fire heat the area, giving it time to charge and cleanse the space.

The Campfire Meditation does not have to be performed only while camping, though it is best used for longer outdoor stints and is best performed at night. It requires more devotion.

1. Build a fair-sized fire and light it with flint rocks, a magnifying glass, or matches. (If experienced enough, try rubbing sticks together, but note that this method requires a lot of skill and strength.)

2. Stand before the flames with your chosen stick. Stare into the center of the blaze. Get close enough to stir the coals when necessary, but not too close.

3. Watch the embers fly up into the sky. Breathe in the cleansing smoke. Feel the connection between the cooling night and the heat of all energy sources.

4. Listen to the fire whisper. Taste its smoky flavor. Focus on the fire as if it is the only other creature in the world.

5. As the wood burns, examine how the flames move and change. Extend the stick into the fire and stir the wood to keep it burning. Imagine the power of the heat at the center. Visualize that energy climbing the stick until it touches palms. Absorb it.

6. Kneel before the fire. Bow to it. Let the energy that has been received wash over the entire body. It will offer a sense of understanding, purpose, or deep connection to the present and the environment.

7. Meditate on that sensation until the fire begins to die down. Then get up and repeat this process for as long as possible.

BONFIRE MEDITATION

Bonfires possess many purposes for Pagans and spiritualists. They aid farmers and communities with a way to return brush clippings back to the earth. They gift healers with purification and new energies. They offer rituals light, guidance, and increased strength. Best done in a clearing surrounded by trees, these larger fires connect people to others as well as the land and their instincts.

There are many options for successful bonfire meditations: they can be done at each person's discretion at random intervals, together as a single group, or in sectioned-off smaller groups with more personal focus. Regardless of the route taken, the steps are simple and effective:

1. Have everyone involved place at least one twig, stick, or branch into the wood pile before lighting the fires.

2. Designate one person to watch over the fire and all involved in case of emergency. This person should be the main one to set it, but others can help light the wood from all around it.

3. Leave plenty of space for safety but circle around the fire. Join hands if you are in a group, or raise your hands to the sky if in smaller sects or alone. Feel the heat build. Listen to the fire pop and crackle. Breathe it

in. Let the energies of everyone present and the space surrounding the fire come together.

4. Chant, hum, or dance before the blaze. Allow the internal energies to reach out to those rising into the air. As the flames pulse, the rhythm should match it until a great buzzing or tingling climaxes all around. When it grows to the point of pure exhilaration, stop and sit down. Close your eyes and hold out your hands.

5. What hidden answers are surfacing from within? How do the other participants' energies mingle together? Recognize, appreciate, and explore these ties in a dreamlike trance.

6. When a rush of goose bumps or cold air awakens, bow to the fire and thank it for the experience.

Natural Body of Water Meditations

Water covers most of the planet. It makes up most of the human body and is crucial to the survival of nearly every living creature on this planet. It not only nourishes life—it also sets forth the cycle that ensures a continuous, connected timeline.

Beyond food and drink, water hosts deeper ties to the spiritual self. In addition to being a necessity for bodily survival, it is also a force that sets us on the right course. It represents the power of acceptance and change. It is everything we often wish to be: powerful, graceful, beautiful, and purposeful.

To achieve spiritual depth, we must strengthen the bond between ourselves and the natural waters that help us thrive. And to do that, we must seek out freshwater springs, ponds, lakes, creeks, gulfs, seas, and oceans to swim in the current of possibilities. If you are unable to do so, a backyard pond, a puddle, or even a trip to a botanical garden can offer similarly potent opportunities for meditation and spiritual growth. For those who are physically unable, it is possible to modify these mediations to be done with basins of water or visualization.

Seeking out wild waters in any setting is a journey that signals a new call. From the smallest sources to the ongoing currents of mighty oceans, these places are where people become part of the greater work.

CREEK/STREAM MEDITATION

Every water source comes from somewhere. It is connected to the cycle that keeps this planet balanced and hydrated. Creeks and streams hold the lighter aspects of H_2O. Some are fed from lakes or artificial structures to direct the force of water away from homes, roads, and businesses.

The most important bodies of water are ones fed from springs. Freshwater springs are living embodiments of the fountain of youth. In our modern age, not enough people have had the opportunity or the courage to experience the rush of cupping one's hands and drinking cool water infused with minerals brought forth by nature alone. It is a divine experience, one that draws forth a sense of power and achievement.

For the following creek/stream meditation, it is recommended to find a freshwater spring to practice this technique, if you are able. If not, any creek or small stream will do.

1. Hike to the small water source. The exertion will clear the mind and prepare the body for what it needs.

2. When reaching the creek or stream, find the most secluded point where the water moves fastest.

3. Stop on the bank and sit, stand, or kneel. Watch the rushing water. See its bubbling motion. Think of how blood rushes through veins and purifies itself in a similar manner. Remove all foot coverings— shoes, boots, socks.

4. Walk into the water just to your ankles. Let it chill your feet and toes. Look down. Visualize the water within your body.

5. Now walk to the deepest point. Trust the natural currents within the self. Cup your hands and dip them into the most active space of water and drink. Taste the earth. Feel the liquid spreading through the system.

6. Walk back to the bank and sit with your feet in the water. Visualize where the water flows. Imagine it connecting to larger bodies and eventually the ocean. Think of all water as one, almost like a living entity. Each drop, each splash, moves back from whence it came. Use that knowledge and that imagery to place the self within that context.

POND MEDITATION

Ponds host an ethereal air. Quiet and calm, they are not as bubbly and loud as other bodies of water. They rest. Waiting for their turn to speak, they are a perfect place for solitude. Wildlife flocks to ponds and brings with it the music of life. Throughout history, humans have used ponds for bathing, fishing, swimming, and more.

Connecting to the calmer waters draws out the past and future while sitting in the present. The pond meditation has two options for practice: in the water while swimming, or in a boat atop smaller, swampier ponds.

1. Wade into the water or push a boat into it and get in. Watch the ripples flow outward.

2. Focus on those ripples and the images that distort upon the mirrored surface of the water.

3. Visualize life as a series of ripples and follow them. Where do they lead?

4. Glide along the water. (Float on your back and swim, or row the boat slowly.)

5. Trust in the power of balance required to float. Trust in the necessity of self-preservation.

6. Stop moving. Let the water carry everything where it will. (If in a boat, dangle hand over side in the water.) Absorb the water's nutrients.

7. Swim or row however you please—water is a playful element. Learn from that.

RIVERS AND LAKES MEDITATION

Larger freshwater sources like rivers and lakes provide a more adventurous connection to the instinctual self. The churning flow makes swimming and fishing more of a challenge, but when practiced correctly the rewards are often greater than those of calmer waters.

It takes care and knowledge to receive the full returns of a river or lake. One must be strong of body and mind if they wish to perform the rivers and lakes meditation. Only strong swimmers and those well versed in wild excursions should engage in this exercise, as it requires one to go underwater.

Before engaging, get to know the area, and do not attempt the exercise during flooding or other unfavorable conditions.

1. Hike around the area surrounding the lake or river. Get to know it if you are not already acquainted. Choose a day with good conditions in a favorable time of year such as during summer when it is less hazardous.

2. Approach the bank or beach. Prepare to swim and walk toward the water, while clearing your mind.

3. Walk into the river or lake. Get a feel for the movements of the current. Get to know the will of the waters.

4. Swim around for a while. Exert the body while observing the surrounding area and the nearby wildlife. Be conscious of breathing.

5. Take a deep breath in preparation for underwater meditation. Sink underwater putting your legs in sitting position or pulling your knees to your chest. Use your arms to stay underwater.

6. Close your eyes, and let the water drown out the world. Hear the whoosh of the current, the rumble of the waves. Absorb everything.

7. Find comfort in blocking out the sense of sight and smell. Focus on feeling. How does the water feel? Your body? How do the two connect?

8. Come up for air when needed and repeat until the water takes on a new light.

OCEAN MEDITATION

My own ocean experiences are restricted by travel because I do not live near an ocean and must journey to them. The largest waters hold many hopes for humanity. For the swimmer entering them, it takes a love of exploration and the unknown to face creatures hiding beneath the surface. Oceans often represent faith. They hold the key to our origins and—if one believes—our creator(s) drifts within the currents. There are ways to see beyond the boundaries of reality through salt water.

The Ocean Meditation can be done in different ways. One can step into the water and float atop it, or submerge themselves completely (use goggles for submersion). No matter how it is done, a person will receive the equivalent sensations of what they put into the waters.

1. Approach the water. Place one foot in and one foot out. The "dry" foot may get wet as the waves roll in but when they pull back it should be untouched.

2. Feel the contrast of the sand grains on the bottom of the feet opposing the air and water that glide over the top.

3. Put both feet in the water. Imagine the depths this great force reaches, and how close the beach is to countless unseen creatures and underwater wonders. Think of how endless the ocean seems, how it connects to the distance of outer space and time.

4. If you are not going in further, sit and let the waves splash against the body. Place your hands atop the water and let the waters move them as they will. Or go further in and float. Trust the water to protect, to guide. Close your eyes and visualize the power of the waves reaching inside your body. Let them rock the pulse and dance with internal currents.

5. If not going under, float or sit until the body tingles and ears ring. A vision of a great water god, spirit, or apparition may reveal itself. Do not fear it. It is always there. If going under, flip after floating and dive down as deep as is comfortable. Pop ears to adjust for pressure and hold breath as long as possible.

6. Look into the endless water. Watch the sunbeams strike through in shifting patterns. Allow your vision to defocus, but keep the mind free. Watch any oncoming movement. Feel the protection of the ocean. The blanket of comfort that drowns out the rest of the world. Get wrapped in it until having to resurface for air. A vision of a water god, spirit, or apparition may make itself known and possibly provide a sense of knowledge that leads to new ideas.

2
GARDENING

No matter the range or scope of one's purpose, long-term satisfaction develops for those who put in as much of themselves as they take out. Gardening prepares people for failure, success, and everything that comes with tending their own affairs. It requires true commitment and the proper tools. Seeds must be obtained in addition to the knowledge of when and how to best plant them.

Not everything grows at the same time. Like humans, plants sprout at different intervals. From gardenias, hyacinths, and magnolias to indoor bamboo and cacti that require little skill for growing, all purify the air while offering natural beauty. These specific options host the power to connect us to good fortune or turn our luck around.

The more fruitful gardens supply nourishment from herbs, spices, and vegetables. Knowing where my food comes from, how it is grown, and how the seed feels when planted brings me closer to the source of my survival. The knowledge reaches into my mind and implants greater connections.

Everything a person consumes affects their being. Nothing tastes better than the freshly picked fruits of your own labor. No air smells sweeter than when supplied by flowers grown with your own two hands. It does not matter how "green" a person's thumb is. Growing and/or tending plant life opens up the senses. It leads the way to new forms of self-awareness and magic.

Indoor Gardening

There are plenty of ways for city dwellers or people who are renting or occupying smaller spaces to grow their own plants. Simple household plants deliver a better connection to the outdoors even when busy lifestyles, ailments, disabilities, or age prevents us from venturing outside.

Often easy to tend, all indoor plants require is a pot, some soil, a little water, and maybe a window if direct sunlight is needed for proper growth. For those wishing to substitute store-bought herbs and foods with home grown foods, indoor gardening is still an option. Celery stalks, lettuces, and tomatoes grow easily indoors. Window sill herb gardens flourish with variety and nutrients.

For the more dedicated who wish to attempt a full-blown indoor garden, lighting substitutes are now readily available with hydroponic options and more. This method takes a lot of time and care but is known to be a potential aid to ensure a brighter future no matter what kind of environmental catastrophes descend upon humanity.

However you choose to garden indoors, there are many rewards. Even a single potted plant can filter air, brighten up a space, and produce a more calming atmosphere. When I lived in a small apartment, it was all I needed.

Growing even just a small herb garden increases physical health. Knowing what you consume from seed to stalk and beyond can provide control over your diet, something of benefit to many homes nowadays. When an individual takes control of the foods they consume, they take control of their life, their personal energies, and their connection to the planet. If growing herbs in this manner is not possible, there are other outward benefits to growing plants indoors.

Plants clean the air. As concerns about pollution exist everywhere, purified air is a gift. The lungs respond better to filtered air. The heart becomes healthier, and blood flow and skin become healthier as a result.

The benefits of fresh air help ease the mind. When we can breathe deeper and receive the full effects of proper airflow, we can better manage our pain, thoughts, and actions.

Indoor plants help motivate people. They do not require as much time and energy as farming or backyard gardening, making them a perfect option for people with tight schedules, illnesses, diseases, disabilities, issues from aging, and so on.

For Mental Health

Too often, people focus on what is missing. While it is a survival skill ingrained in us based on genetic memory and instinct, that instinct snowballed into something different at some point in the shift to the Industrial Age. It became far more detrimental than helpful. It is thus important for us to step away from our troubles into a neutralized scenario in order to find a place of heightened mental control.

Plant life is a perfect neutralizer to the pains of the world. Plants represent healing powers. Despite the fact that some are poisonous to eat, can mar the skin or spread rashes, or even cause death, the seeds of the future rest inside the fruits of today.

Through indoor gardening, it is easy to find your internal nurturer without having the mess of training a pet or chasing after children. There is reduced stress in an enclosed environment that provides potential for accurate hypotheses.

The best way to clear the mind of negative thoughts and imbalances is to obtain and keep stable representations of positive outcomes, balance, and comfort in one's home. Indoor gardens do this perfectly.

To start:

1. Determine how much space is available for an indoor plant or garden (and if planning a detailed design, research it beforehand).
2. Find a nursery, gardening center, or online seed bank to obtain the right plant(s).
3. Dig in. Get the garden planted.
4. Water as needed. Place near window as needed. Talk to the plant. Don't be afraid to touch the soil, stalk, or blooms once fully matured.
5. Meditate on the garden or plant. Even just five minutes of sitting before it and thinking of its progress will offer a sense of peace and purpose.

For Spiritual Health

Indoor gardening is a living embodiment of spiritual perseverance. A plant cannot speak of its needs. It cannot gesture like animals, but it expresses itself in other ways.

Without help, indoor plants shrivel from lack of nourishment, much like people display unhealthy outward appearances when they are not receiving the proper nutrients for their being. The two phenomena are directly linked—our souls thrive when our environment is suited to our needs.

My own struggle with planting and mental health issues seemed all too linked when I first opened myself up to gardening. When I found myself in a mania and focused on music or painting, I would forget my plants and their needs. As my body shifted and my mood dipped low, I just gave up on trying to revive them. All it took were some hardy plants who refused to die to give me the confidence I needed to let the connection grow and thrive.

As the spiritual link thickens, meditations evolve into spellwork, and spellwork is the spirits' voice to reach the universe. The secrets of the spirit world will open to those who reach out. Being fully connected to everything around us on a higher level (beyond the external) thins that barrier.

To build a deeper bond with a full garden or even a single plant, test out a few practices:

1. Meditate with or on the plant for longer periods.

2. During this time, open the senses and clear the mind of all other thought.

3. Focus on sight first (it is easiest). Stare at the plant. Study every detail. See the life as an integral aspect of the planet's survival.

4. Close your eyes, and focus on hearing. Plants do not have verbal abilities—a lesson for us in itself. Let the stillness be a friend. Do not play any kind of media in the background. Give in to the silence and imagine how the world grew for thousands of years in this kind of quiet long before modern noise.

5. Keep your eyes closed. Breathe in and focus on whatever you smell. The scent of dirt and earthy aromas should grace your olfactory prowess. If you are growing floral vegetation, admire the sweet perfume in the air.

6. Again keeping the eyes closed, reach for the plant with soft hands. Brush it with your fingertips and gently rub leaves or petals between the thumb and forefinger. Every living thing on this planet releases

powerful chemicals when touched. Absorb that great healing energy and be content.

7. This may be a bit much for some but if you are willing, keep your eyes closed and grab a small piece of the dirt and place it on your tongue. Swallow it. There is more power in that small bite of soil than in an entire of a society of people who do not know how to grow anything.

Porch/Deck Gardening

For those who have no yard space to plant extravagant flower beds or vegetable gardens but at least a deck or porch space, smaller outdoor gardens contain many possibilities. Hanging planters, garden boxes, and pots can set the scene for abundant greenery.

Smaller, enclosed garden planters are the perfect place for annual flowers that spring up at different intervals throughout the year. Depending on the climate of the location, leafy bushes, small trees, or shrubs might be a proper addition. If the seasons meet extreme weather, plants with longer lives can be both indoor and outdoor/deck growths that serve multiple purposes.

Filling large pots, baskets, and/or boxes with soil and tending it while growing a small outdoor garden holds many of the benefits of indoor planting but also the added benefits of fresh air, unfiltered sunlight, and a stronger sense of community, as well as bird watching and wildlife connections. All of these activities draw forth heightened energy levels.

Stepping outside to enjoy the sprouts that color the areas around an apartment, condo, townhome, or studio delivers a reprieve. It provides sanctuary. Even in the most overcrowded cities, a small porch garden reminds us of plants' significance. That sense grows along with the seeds. It binds us to the area surrounding us with a stronger appreciation of what we have.

Determining how much time can be devoted to this endeavor is the first step. Once that is decided, obtaining the proper materials is next. The cost of this venture can seem astronomical, but there are always better ways. Reusing or recycling materials that would otherwise be thrown away is one of the easiest and most productive methods for saving money and helping the environment. Egg cartons are perfect for growing seedlings. Old plastic containers can be painted and repurposed as pots. Glasses and dishes have many uses for growing.

Seeds can be purchased, found, or gifted; however this small garden forms, it belongs to its creator and will reflect their inner workings.

If plants grow well, so will people. This is a good philosophy to uphold when looking at the physical benefits of small gardening endeavors. Humanity's direct relationship to health and gardening is unarguable. In areas where less plant life is found, people are more likely to develop lung cancers and other circulatory system related complications.

Cities and compact suburbs have their benefits. They make it easier to communicate with others and find goods and services closer to homes and communities. I loved it when I was in early adulthood. It was a perfect setting with lots of excitement. Just a few green friends reminded me that nature is with me always.

To aid the body in this lifestyle, porch or deck gardens purify the air, and get people outside and moving around. Herbs, select vegetables, and a few fruits can be grown with limited space. From basil to mint, an endless list of garden herbs are available for small scale planting. Tomatoes are well-known for growing easily in a pot or hanging planter. Even strawberries can thrive in more controlled garden.

For Mental Health

Just having a place to sit and be thankful each day improves mental health. It lends perspective on the human condition and reminds individuals that no matter how insignificant they sometimes feel, there is always at least one creature dependent upon their connection.

Flexibility is required to determine how best to set up a small outdoor garden. When something goes wrong, it should not be taken as defeat but lead to new vines.

Unlike the indoor garden, all the required elements are readily available. They may not be overly abundant, but their presence is enough to solidify a space. To do so:

1. Cleanse the area. This can be done by burning sage, singing, chanting, or meditating in the spot where the small garden will be placed.

2. Get the pots, baskets, boxes, or other holders ready. While doing so, imagine what will grow best from the containers in the area.

3. Once the seeds, sprouts, or full plants are obtained, transport them to the new garden. Don't be afraid to talk to them, sing, chant, or whisper. Singing is less conspicuous to neighbors.

4. While planting and transplanting look to the ground beneath. Glance at the sky above. Take a moment to scan the entire area beyond the deck or porch. Visualize how it would look untouched by modern society. Think back to what it must have been like a hundred, two hundred, three hundred years ago. Then thank the universe for the opportunity to plant.

5. Once all the roots and seeds are covered, sit in the center of the garden. Close your eyes. Breathe in deep. Feel the force of the new lives surrounding the space. Welcome them. Be grateful for them.

6. Visit the garden at least once a day. Don't be afraid to talk or sing to the plants. Touch them. Meditate on them and beside them.

For Spiritual Health

Small gardens hold rewards and appeal for all types of people. Even those with allergies or medical sensitivities can potentially work with plants that do not inflame any symptoms because it is done on a smaller scale in a more controlled environment. Spiritual heath thrives when we care for a small garden, and it offers a perfect cover to go out during the full moon and become closer with the creator(s) without interference.

To truly enjoy the spiritual benefits of a small deck or porch garden:

1. Arrange the plants to offer more privacy on full moon night.

2. Go out and absorb the illumination. Stand before the plants and see how the soft light brings out new shades of possibilities.

3. Slowly kneel and examine every shadow. Some may reveal new ideas, thoughts, or buds.

4. Gaze up at the sky when a warm sense of peace seems to coat your body. Stand and bow.

Community Gardening

Community plots where neighbors come together to work the land are becoming more common each year. These gardens provide a place for everyone to work with at their own pace and also share tips and find common ground. Society's ties to farming and food is not forgotten. The community garden creates a new association, giving people a place to combine their knowledge and put it to good use for the benefit of everyone.

Finding a community garden is as simple as doing an online search or asking around. Neighbors are usually eager to open up about them. I learned about the opportunity from a flyer and then discussed it with neighbors before joining. It took some effort to get started, but that effort paid off.

If a garden space has yet to be created in a city or populated suburb, anyone can start one. All that's needed is to contact your local government, usually a Parks services or Community office or similar. It's usually a good idea to speak with neighbors to get support before asking the city. If funding or space is not available, fundraisers, donations, or joining a nearby community garden outside of your neighborhood are other options for making this a reality if you are interested and passionate about the prospect.

Physical health and a connection to the earth go hand in hand. Ramps, benches, and handrails can be installed to accommodate everyone. Community gardens are designed to be centrally located on a plot of land that anyone can get to with or without a vehicle. They offer sunlight and peace, a perfect balance for physical health. There are many different ways to find enjoyment in physicality. Everyone has varying interests and likes. Community gardening is just one example of a simple route that can lead to balanced energies. There is magic within those energies.

For Mental Health

Community gardens remind us of our humanity. When a person steps out of their house to greet their neighbors and do their part to achieve a same or similar goal, common ground develops. Understanding is more easily achieved on a smaller scale. Reaching out to each other helps prevent and ease conflicts.

When these tension building aspects of life are lessened the mind is better able to cope with stress and painful events. Fresh air and sunshine remind gardeners of the simple things that equalize us. What is planted and how it is tended is where individuality lets neighbors stand out with their own taste and styles.

It is not always easy to leave the house and enter the community. Face-to-face interactions are more meaningful and therefore possess more consequences. Depending on the nature of the area and situation, it may take multiple visits to feel welcome or productive. Even just visiting the plants or reading to the bees reminds humans of what has been missing.

To find good mental health practices within community gardening:

1. Acknowledge any fears, doubts, concerns. Meditate on being confident and trying hard.

2. Join a community garden and go to a designated plot or area that needs tending. Connect with the tasks and let them occupy your mind. Everything else will slip away as the work is done.

3. If others are nearby, introduce yourself or at least offer a wave or a nod, maybe a smile. This is where real life interactions matter most. These are things our ancestors did for thousands of years. Do them justice and break free from the invisible chains that have formed in this strange age of overcommunicators who do not truly communicate.

4. Take a moment to close your eyes and sniff the air. Listen to the sounds of the garden. Open the sense to feel the magnitude of the energy surrounding the area and get acquainted with it.

For Spiritual Health

A confined spirit cannot breathe properly. No matter how comfortable a person is with their living space, the outdoors beckon. They reach out.

Community gardens offer a unique space to pour our energy into the land, transform it, and receive it anew. This opens the heart and pushes our being beyond just the physical aspects of life. The dirt, the earth, the plants and all the insects within the garden all display purpose.

There is nothing more sacred than the spaces that provide nourishment. This garden will be blessed with struggle and joy. It is a proper place to feel safe, to open up, and to sprinkle the seeds of new possibilities.

Working within a community strengthens the spirit mainly because it forces even the shyest people to step out of the shadows and let their light shine for

everyone to see. It also stands to humble those who believe they are more important than others. It aids in the journey of figuring out the balance between being
an individual while also enjoying a role as a part of the entirety of humanity.

To open up the spirit and allow it to speak within a community garden:

1. This step is best done alone, in trusted company, or when planting
   while no one is looking. Consecrate the ground with an offering,
   whether it is blood from scratched hands after digging, spit, sweat,
   a hair from your head, or an offering of food.

2. Dig until your hands can be buried. Let them sit under the cool soil.
   Feel its simplicity, its potential.

3. Breathe in the smell of earth. Meditate on the area. Imagine how vast
   the underground world is. Think of the roots that lie hidden beneath
   the surface of the planet. Imagine the animals and insects that reside
   unseen.

4. Bow to the land that will be cultivated.

Backyard Gardening/Farming

Large scale gardening and farming is a hefty topic. Some people are born in
farmland and therefore have a better understanding of this complex practice
while others have little to no knowledge of backyard gardening or farming. It is
possible to learn as you go no matter which route is taken. What's most important is getting to know the land. Walk the grounds. Take note of wildlife patterns. Find the best spot for full sun.

Sometimes having a partner or farmhand to do the legwork helps when ailments or physical issues catch up with us. Pictures, video, and advice from a trusted
helper is another way to keep connected when our bodies create difficulties.

Once an understanding of the space has been established, planning what
to grow comes next. Location, climate, and personal preference all need to be
taken into consideration before any seeds have been obtained. Determine what
will grow in abundance, what may need more work, and what is unrealistic.
Figure out the size and shape of the space that will be used.

Backyard gardening does not require as much time as farming. My own
vegetable garden does not take up my entire backyard but still produces ample

crops. It takes as little as an hour or two once a week for me to plant and care for vegetables that come up.

Growing a vegetable garden or farming the old-fashioned way (without harmful chemicals and extreme conditions) contributes to overall health greatly. The process taps into our deeper selves and can be explored further if we are conscious of the meaning; self-reliance and simplistic prosperity heal many wounds. Maintaining a constant willingness to learn leads to inner peace and enlightenment. It is also a gateway to the gods/the universe and the possibilities beyond.

Proper food fuels the body so it can grow, heal, and carry out necessary tasks as well as recreational ones. Large scale gardening and farming has much to supply for overall health. There is nothing better for a person than fresh natural fruits and vegetables and the work required to cultivate them.

For Mental Health

Growing backyard crops or tending a farm gets a person out of the main frequency range. It reduces the need to concern ourselves with what others are doing, allowing us to focus on our own meaningful tasks in the moment. Too often people worry about the past and the future instead of finding joy in the little things that make the present a true experience.

Disconnecting from the bigger picture can actually give someone the power they need to do more good for the greater purpose. It lends insight to the mind.

The following will help you generate a mindful backyard garden or farm that supports better thinking and mental health:

1. Stand in the middle of the garden/farm beside a row (so as not to disturb any plants).
2. Close your eyes. Bring your arms up and reach to the sky. Breathe deep.
3. Open your eyes and look up at the sky. Think of the air surrounding everyone, every plant.
4. Close your eyes again and reach down as far as possible. Breathe deep.
5. Open your eyes and look at the soil. Think of the plants growing from it.
6. Stand up and once again close your eyes. Reach your arms out to each side. Breathe deep.
7. One last time, open your eyes and feel the importance of being alive.

For Spiritual Health

For those who love the outdoors, backyard gardening and farming is a gift that eases the mind and also has a profound effect on the spirit and the energies within.

Working with numerous plants takes patience and care and brings out higher energies. A person can achieve more than they believed was possible beforehand. When drought or flooding occurs, it challenges our usual methods and calls on us to find other means. The instincts that rest dormant in those who easily find ingredients at the store come alive in the field.

From those instincts comes power and electricity. When harnessed, the soul hums, the body sings.

Anyone can grow something, but it takes dedication and practice to instigate further change. Nudging the elements that make up the world around us is possible when we call upon our internal knowledge and forget society's rules that constrain us.

Nurturing growth is a process. It takes multiple attempts, failure, and success. Disappointment must give way to the goal. Here's a good place to start:

1. Fill an open watering can or bowl with water and bring it to the garden or center of the farm. Sit in between rows and place your fingertips on the surface of the water. Feel its energy, its purpose.

2. Now clear your mind. Focus on your life source. Where does it come from? The head and the heart are the most commonly recognized. Wherever the center of the energy within is generated, place your hand over it while plunging the other hand in the water.

3. Focus on the link between life and water. Visualize your energies going into the water and returning anew.

4. Now place both hands atop the dirt. Skim your fingertips over the soil. Feel its energy, its purpose.

5. Again, clear the mind. Dig with your hands until there is enough earth to cover one hand. Let your fingernails get dirty, do not be afraid of soiled skin. Bury the hand that went underwater. Place the hand that did not get submerged upon the source of the energy within you.

6. Focus on the link between life and the soil. Visualize your energies going into the ground and returning anew.

7. Raise your arms to the sky and close your eyes. Feel the powers combining. Think of your ancestors who lived closer to nature and how their spirits must have felt. Imagine a future where that connection is restored. Visualize your place in that future.

8. Call upon the elements to aid you. Thank the gods/the universe for the means.

Spells

Spellwork is like physical prayer. A person must put in the effort and solidify it with their energies. The more realistic the request or desire, the more successful a spell can be.

GROWTH SPELL

(To aid a plant or garden in its growth)

MATERIALS NEEDED: Self, the plant or garden

TO PREPARE: Meditate on the plant or in front of the garden: first clear the mind, then focus on connecting energies between yourself and the living being(s) that will be affected.

THE WORK:

1. Place hands at the roots of the plant or soil above the planted seed during the end of meditation.

2. Visualize it growing full and luscious.

3. Imagine the feel of its full potential as if it were already grown.

4. Let that sensation build throughout the entire body as if connected and charged with an electric current.

5. Take one fingertip and draw the image of strong, healthy roots flowing from the sprout or soil where the seed is planted. Then raise that fingertip and draw the fully grown plant above the soil.

6. Bow to the earth and thank it for its power. Then lie back and ground your body in reality. Feel the energies wane and rebalance. Any light-headedness should dissipate. Your body should feel relaxed.

GARDEN FERTILITY SPELL

(For a plant, animal, or person)

MATERIALS NEEDED: An egg, bowl of food scraps, and the subject

TO PREPARE: Collect leftovers and food scraps in a bowl for at least a week before the rite, if not an entire moon cycle (this will be an offering to the earth energies). Just before the rite, meditate on the subject, first clearing the mind, and then focusing on connecting energies between the self and the living being(s) that will be affected. (This is a great self-spell for women looking to start a family.)

THE WORK:

1. Carry the bowl to the outdoor garden or large indoor potted plant. Kneel and set the bowl down.

2. Place hands over the leftovers and envision them going back to the earth as an offering. If compelled to do so chant or sing.

3. Dig a hole large enough for the food offering and place the leftovers into the soil, leaving the hole open.

4. When ready, take the egg in hands. Hold over the bowl and visualize a healthy creature forming without complications.

5. Bring the egg close to heart and rock it as if it were a baby. Kiss it. Welcome protection and guidance for the life that is to be.

6. Crack the egg over the food offering in the soil. Crush the shell in your hands and place beside the egg atop the food.

7. Cover everything with dirt while envisioning a healthy new life. It may take up to a month to fulfill but should come to be.

8. Bow to the earth and thank it for its power. Then lie back and ground your body in reality. Feel the energies wane and rebalance. Any light-headedness should dissipate. Your body should feel relaxed.

GARDEN FIRE SPELL

(To purify and focus)

Materials Needed: Dried stalks and garden clippings. Firepit or space. Matches, flint rocks, or other fire starter

To Prepare: This spell is good to do under a new moon. Prune and preen the garden. Collect clippings and leave them to dry out over days, weeks, or moths depending on outdoor climate.

The Work:

1. Before the sun goes down, collect sticks and twigs on the grounds or nearby.

2. Line the bottom of the fire pit or space with the longest, straightest wood.

3. Place garden clippings on top of the wood, building them up pointing toward the center like a pyramid.

4. Kneel before the dried plants. Bow to their sacrifice. Say a few words or chant a phrase recognizing the importance of loss, how it purifies what remains and forces it to focus.

5. Ignite the dried plants. Get up and follow the smoke if it twists away. Sit in the cloud with eyes closed. Let it wash away the past and recharge the future.

6. Feel the energies inside build. Your head may tingle; let that feeling spread. Give in.

7. Open eyes. As the clippings burn up, throw in the rest of the sticks and twigs one at a time. Meditate on each stick as it goes in.

8. Bow to the fire and thank it for its power. Then lie on the grass or dirt beside the fire as it dies and ground your body in reality. Feel the energies wane and rebalance. Any lightheadedness should dissipate. Your body should relax.

CORN DOLL SPELL FOR CHANGE

(To improve one's self)

Materials Needed: Corn husks. Bowl of water. Toothpicks or small twigs, string, yarn, or long grasses, fire pit or space for a fire, matches or other fire source

To Prepare: Harvest corn. Keep the husks and tassels. Soak in water.

The Work:

1. Best started during the August ritual and finished on the first day of autumn. Take the soaked husks and tassels from water. Curl, wind, or ball them into body parts and make a doll that represents yourself. Use twigs or toothpicks with string or grasses to assemble.

2. Meditate on the doll. Close your eyes and visualize the energies within connecting to the doll in your hands. Now think of all bad habits, issues, and character flaws you wish to improve or eliminate. Push those images into the doll. Think of each limb as a place to store those defects so you can become a well-rounded individual.

3. Keep the doll until Mabon/the autumn equinox. During the interval meditate on the doll, remembering to expel the issues you wish to be rid of.

4. During or after the fall ritual, create a fire and stand before it with the corn doll. Hug it. Kiss its face. Accept love from yourself and say goodbye to the parts that you wish to move on from.

5. Gently place the doll in the fire and watch it burn. Feel the change within. Stand tall and raise arms to the sky. Chant or say a few words about walking forward with a new air.

KITCHEN/GARDEN PROTECTION SPELL

(To protect yourself or loved ones, especially children)

Materials Needed: A recently baked good; an item of importance to whomever will receive the protection (like a book or toy); area to bury the baked item; a small bowl; garden shovel; matches, sticks, twigs, and logs for fire

To Prepare: On the day of the full moon, bake a treat: bread, muffins, or similar. Have the person needing the protection present for the mixing. If possible, have them stir at least once before the dough is baked. Bake as usual. Wait until night to perform the spell.

THE WORK:

1. Gather one baked item for each person to be protected. For example, if the spell is for yourself, use one good. For three children, three goods. Place them all in a small bowl.

2. Go to the garden under the full moon's light (or bring potted plant outside) with the bowl of baked items, a shovel, the item that represents the person to be protected, and the materials for the fire.

3. Kneel before the garden. Dig one hole per person/good. Think of the person needing the protection while digging.

4. Place the food into the hole(s), one at a time. Take a small handful of dirt and place it in the bowl. Use the rest to fill in the hole and bury the offering. The place the item that represents the person on top of the burial site, one at a time. (Starting and finishing each hole and placing the item before moving to the next if doing multiples.)

5. Look to the moon. Thank her for her light. Ask her to provide protection for the subject(s).

6. Take the bowl of dirt to fire space. Build a fire and ignite it. Take the bowl of dirt and throw it into the fire one handful at a time, looking to the moon and then the flames.

7. Thank the fire for its warmth. Ask it to provide protection for the subject(s).

8. Kneel to the flames. Meditate and feel the power of the spell. Visualize it weaving around the area and through the offering(s) in the garden.

3
HIKING

Exploration is embedded in humanity. Some creatures stick to one territory and others migrate over certain distances, but humans are unique in our constant quest to seek out new lands.

Where this desire for adventure comes from is unknown, though it's possible our thought processes and skills may have led to it. In conjunction with this primal instinct, walking affords people satisfaction in regards to exploration and adventure. Traveling along footpaths and bridges, on sidewalks, or even the shoulder of a road slows down the busy world. It reconnects us to the lands we pass by.

Being conscious of where I am going—not just physically but how the destination and reaching it affects my thoughts and physicality—draws out a more meaningful journey. That bond is what calls to the energies within. It gives a voice to instincts and can even sway the universe.

When wandering through fields, hidden wildlife invigorates my senses. Grasses and vegetation inspire. The scenery spells out my specific needs more clearly. Sometimes the elements, gods, or the universe whispers directly in this setting. I often find messages hiding in the trees, and it is here I am the most open to listening and changing.

Forests especially host spiritual guidance. Emerald lands full of trees, mosses, mushrooms, and ivy reveal their most treasured wildlife, when I let go of my problems and find patience with life. Mountain air challenges my lungs, but also gifts me with accomplishment. Climbing a mountain takes determination. The act itself serves as a work to increase external understanding.

By contrast, hiking deserts and beaches hones in on personal power. The friction of sand against body weight adds a difficulty that serves as a reminder that we are more than the physical structure that supports us. The waters that lap at the shore under the endless sky of a beach speak of truths stored within. Blowing winds that whistle against countless grains and dance with dunes in scorching deserts impart their wisdom. Honor and compassion surface when we accept these messages. Tapping into my surroundings for the betterment of myself allows me to become more balanced so I can help others and extend that energy to the world.

Lastly, hiking through caves always left me in awe as a child; I remember once walking carefully with my mother on a guided tour. The open world of easy sensory perception shifted, and I had to find a way to trust myself and those around me when passing through the enclosed networks of the unknown.

The mind expands and relaxes in the moment once comfortable in a dark recess. Instead of expecting a cheap thrill, childlike wonder takes over to provide the ideal setting for spiritual quandaries. Answers echo in the silence and images may flit before flashlights that offer a glimpse of possibility.

All types of hiking deepen the bonds between the spirit and earth, but everyone engaging in such activity must be cautious and travel in groups after notifying others of where they plan to be in case of emergencies. Well-monitored caves housed at public parks are the only safe place to perform the exercises mentioned in this chapter—I do not advise them to be performed elsewhere.

Depending on resources, availability, and will, exploring these routes releases instinctual energies that serve as markers on the map of life, but safety should always be a main focus.

Fields

Easy on the body, field hiking is the easiest option for people seeking a low-impact experience. City parks usually host flat field spaces to welcome a variety of physical levels, and some even include paved walkways for wheelchair access. A few slopes are sometimes encountered, but at a gradual rate. Tracks, trails, and pathways can be found on public land or cleared in private areas.

Field hiking is more in accordance with rhythm than exploration because there is a heightened visibility range. That rhythm harbors energy that synchronizes one's presence with the creatures inhabiting the space. A network of unseen adventure awaits.

Because it is difficult to get lost in a field, this is a good place for starters—paths that wind through these tall grasses do not disappoint. They are a perfect space to extend your hands and brush your skin against the plants beneath them. To connect further (and if it is safe to do so), step off the path. When surrounded by wild vegetation and the numerous insects feeding off the land, the bigger picture is clear.

Hiking humbles egos. It returns us to a balanced state. And hiking in fields accomplishes this easily due to their vastness. They feed and shelter more creatures than meet the eye while displaying an emptiness on the surface that is easy to relate to.

The simple act of placing one foot in front of the other (literally and figuratively) is the basis for all paths of success. I always keep moving and absorb what is around me when seeking knowledge.

Easy Paths/Trails

The simplicity held within a single meadow reminds people that complexity does not always mean success or beauty. There is a time for relaxation. There is a time for appreciating where one has been before they move on to tackle more difficult challenges. There is a time for meditation before spellwork and grounding after.

Walking the trails that cut through these places requires very little exertion; on days when I'm tired or overworked, the simplicity aids me. It helps me focus more on breathing and opening my lungs to better use my mind.

Human life is impossible without air. Deep breathing exercises strengthen the body and brain while supporting the energies that extend beyond. Deep breathing calms the mind and comforts an individual:

1. Walk along the path. Be conscious of the rhythm of your steps.

2. Take time to breathe. Inhale slowly for as many seconds as possible. Hold the air for a second before slowly exhaling, taking as long as possible.

3. With each breath, focus on a new sight: look first to one side, then the other, forward, down, and up. Look for details that are not apparent upon first glance.

4. Become wholly conscious of the ecosystem and focus on that concept. Each living creature within the field is an individual with their own purpose; at the same time, everything works together like a larger entity.

5. The field may seem as if it is alive, breathing on its own. This is nothing to be feared.

6. Go as far as possible. When finished, bow to the field. Be grateful for its presence and wish it well.

Wildlife

For some, the main thrill of hiking is animal encounters. Unlike playing with pets or observing animals held in zoos, animal refuges, and wildlife rescue centers, the creatures found in fields are truly wild. This can create moments of enlightenment, but also danger.

Plenty of people have walked up to wild animals and been horribly injured by a creature that seemed docile and harmless. When encountering an animal, my instincts are all I have. There are not perfect guidelines to follow for each individual situation because like every person, all animals are different. What has mainly served me well is keeping calm and maintaining a safe distance.

Most animals react based on the behavior and reactions around them, feeding off and responding to the energies surrounding them. If a person shows fear, it will scare the creature. Deep breathing and self-control create better opportunity for calm attitudes in the face of unexpected encounters. These traits develop over time and are sometimes lifesaving when hiking.

There are lots of ways to enhance the instincts linking a person to the wild animals they share the planet with. Learn about movement patterns and the best time of day to spot them. The following are also good practices:

1. Take a hike in a field just before sunrise or sunset.

2. Be quiet. Move slowly. Find a good place to stop and wait.

3. Visualize being the creature you most wish to see. Consider how they often spend long periods of time waiting, camouflaging themselves into their surroundings.

4. Lose track of time. Let the field be your home.

5. It may take a few attempts, but eventually something will reveal itself.

Scenery

The wildflowers and grasses that paint a field are more than just colorful elements that add to the overall aesthetic. When hiking through fields, those who chose to do so can learn about different plant species and benefit from them. Some parks and nature reserves even employ guides who give tours. Individuals with knowledge of what is growing can also spot edible grasses, flowers, and mushrooms with ease.

The exhilaration of consuming earthy onion grass or munching harmless fungus is less about taste and more about the find, the nutrients. Natural foods are often blander because they weren't made to stimulate all the parts of the brain but simply fuel the body. Accepting this and understanding it deepens the experience.

A beautiful aspect of life is the scenery the earth provides. Busy lives leave little time to recognize and absorb the wonders of nature. We must make it a priority if we wish to find inner strength, balance, and instinctual magic.

Hiking to a field does not have to be a full-on spiritual experience—not every excursion allows for that kind of commitment. Even just passing by a park and taking a moment to gaze out over the meadows reveals more about life and myself than other excursions. It reminds me that I do not have to be any one thing; I have many roles I take on at different times. At home, I care for my children and our house. When at festivals or speaking engagements, I am there for the people. When I get lost in beautiful scenery, the experience is truly for me.

A well-rounded person can combine all the roles they must take on in life. This integration is best done through the practices listed here, adding more creative elements that give everything its meaning.

A simple five-minute deep breathing pause can create success in all fields:

1. Walk to the field and stand at its edge.

2. Gaze out over the plants growing; breathe in, deep and slow.

3. See how the plants reach for the sun. Recognize the power in their simplicity and breathe out deep and slow.

4. Find one stalk, leaf, or blossom that stands out. Focus on it and breathe in. Let it represent you.

5. Hold that breath for as long as you can. Feel its pressure, the thumping pulse of momentum that follows.

6. Close your eyes and visualize the pulse of the plant, the field surrounding it, the city, the world and breathe out. See the importance of the self in that great work.

7. Breathe in, ready to meet higher purposes, to take on whatever comes. Greet others. Smile at them. Encourage them in their growth. This will ground the spirit.

More opportunities will come. When longer visits are possible, take a walk through another field or the same one. Really focus on what grows around the trail. Clear the mind and open the senses to the voice of the field.

Breathtaking images deepened with the sun's brilliance remain with us long after we leave. They keep attention spans connected. Taking a picture, or sketching a drawing here and there, stops time and preserves it so one can philosophize further.

Nature art is something that has fallen by the wayside. Talented artists are drowned out by gimmicks and trends. However a person comes to find art in fields, they can remember it (even if they do not have a great memory) through the pieces it inspired. If you are more the analytical type, collecting flowers or other plants for pressing or stones can leave you with a souvenir that can be used for educational purposes or just private satisfaction.

This can be done in any setting, but fields are the main area this is best done in because of good conditions, lighting, etc. Snow topped mountain peaks and shadowy forests host their own energies.

Forests

Each geographical area holds its own unique atmosphere. The elements come together in different ways. Forests are mysterious places. It is easy to get lost within a large network of trees and shade, something that can benefit those who are seeking refuge *or* adventure. Most parks offer trails with different levels of difficulty to accommodate less mobile hikers. Studying maps beforehand is the best way to choose the path that is right for you and your level of physicality.

Tree cover is a sanctuary from modern life. Clean air away from bustling cities restores the body to its best working state. Hiking through the woods explores one's prowess. Some trails are steeper than others, but they all wind through a covered habitat that contains endless life-forms. Observing the diverse ecosystems within a forest leads to insight. Exploring them further rewards some with wisdom.

There is a spirit within these areas. It encompasses visitors and even speaks to those willing to listen. From the tinkle of wind in the treetops to the low tones howling at night, forests have a voice that gives people the ability to speak up for their purpose. Getting to these areas pushes away the excess. We forget all distractions.

Harmony between society and nature can be obtained. There is a balance to be had, but humanity must be willing to compromise. Hiking the great timberlands pushes this idea to the forefront. It shines a light on solutions like the sun beams penetrating the leafy canopy.

Moderate Paths/Trails

Low-impact and moderate hiking trails are in abundance. For well-versed explorers, even what may be considered dangerous or rough terrain can be a "walk in the park" when compared to mountain climbing or much more extreme outdoor activities.

The hiking options within a forest vary. Short and long trails are often offered within the same area to appease a broader network of guests. Mile markers and simplified maps give individuals a glimpse of possible routes to get acquainted with city, state, and national parks. When exploring new property or unknown territory, it is always best to steady one's pace. The unknown is more exhilarating but also perilous.

Walking on overgrown paths or creating new trails takes patience and common sense. It is vital to be aware of what grows around the area. I am highly allergic to poison ivy and it grows everywhere in my area. It loves hot, humid weather almost as much as I do, so I have to watch my step at every turn.

Best done off the trail to avoid unwanted encounters with other people, hiking meditations can be explored as follows:

1. Walk a hiking trail until reaching a spot that refuses to be passed by.

2. Step off the path carefully. Let each footfall land like it is the first step ever taken. Do not venture too far (and risk getting lost), but put at least five to ten trees between the path and the meditation.

3. Sit on the ground with back to a tree. Preferably facing away from the trail.

4. Rest your hands on the ground. Close your eyes and breathe deep. Inhale the intoxicating aroma of bark and mud. Let it clear the perfumes and deodorants of civilization from the mind. Taste the subtlety, the earthy richness.

5. Listen to the woods. Do twigs snap? Do leaves rustle? Are bird calls sent echoing by?

6. Recognize the importance of these sounds. Each reverberation is a song of life and survival.

7. Now think of how the human world contrasts. There is a lot more noise, but not any increase in the message of life or survival. Think about that. Let silent thought hold more meaning than static.

8. Follow the mind on its journey. Then pat the ground and stand up. Turn back toward the path and continue the hike.

Wildlife

Spotting forest wildlife is based on skill level. Plenty of birds and squirrels reveal themselves easily. Chipmunks, woodpeckers, and rabbits can be seen if caught off-guard or a hiker is observant. Other creatures hide. Raccoons, opossums, coyotes, foxes, and deer need cover to adequately find food and safety from larger predators. Nocturnal habits make twilight hikes a better time to potentially come across these animals.

In regards to wolves, moose, cougars, and bears, these great beasts are best found from a distance. An encounter can be peaceful from any position. It depends on the timing and mood. The larger an animal is the more territorial it tends to be. They need more space and they will defend it however they need to.

A person entering any forest should be self-aware. Using all senses will aid you in any journey in the wilderness or even small wooded areas. I often find myself returning to certain areas that call to me. When I revisit places like Rockwood's Reservation or Castlewood State Park in my home state, the friendlier the wildlife seems to be. I bow to them out of respect and carefully observe without interference.

The best way to enjoy the creatures of a forest is to appreciate their freedom. Appreciating a close encounter is simple:

1. Bow to the creature.

2. Watch its movements. Inhale and make sure the space between is safe.

3. Exhale and kneel or sit. Whisper to it. Thank it for allowing your passage.

4. Study the animal's behavior. Many times they are just as curious as we are. As long as they do not feel threatened or are starving, this experience should be positive.

5. If the animal comes closer respond according to the nature of the creature. If they do not get to close, enjoy the moment, forget time. Think of others who may have shared this rare treat.

6. Once alone meditate on what happened. Visualize the scene, the energy, the connectedness.

Plant Life

Familiarizing yourself with what is edible beforehand offers the opportunity for spontaneous snacks. As guests in the forest, we should take not more than a handful; food there is for the wildlife. All the same, connecting with nature through nourishment does bring about a different consciousness.

Gaining a basic knowledge of what to look out for better prepares a hiker so when they come in contact with plants they know what is safe and what is not. Like our ancestors before us, that knowledge turns to wisdom with experience and perspective.

To feed the spirit as well as the body:

1. Step off the trail slowly, and respectfully.

2. Gather a handful of edible berries or mushrooms.

3. Find a space about five to ten trees away to meditate.

4. Sit with your back to the tree, facing away from trail.

5. Cup empty hand over the fuel. Thank the forest for its offering. Close your eyes and open your senses.

6. Place one bite on the tongue. Raw ingredients are not dressed up for the taste buds. Be appreciative no matter how bitter or bland the food is.

7. Eat at your own pace and close your eyes. Visualize the nutrients going into your digestive tract and being dispersed throughout your body.

8. Open your eyes, bow to the land, and get back on the path.

Scenery

Hiking through wooded areas reminds me of my humanity. It is where I find the common ground between living in the technological world and the wild one. Travels to the forests are my way of continuing an ancient rite. Just walking the land gives me power and invigorates me.

Luckily, some modern accommodations have been implemented for those who need assistance. Bridges, rails, benches, and wooden staircases are found across numerous hiking trails. These structures give more people a place to reach out to their instincts and look to nature. The trees jut above. The ground rolls and lumps out of view. Animals go about their routines with caution as they did before recorded history.

Witnessing this firsthand lends one the potential to deepen their understanding of life and creation:

1. Walk a trail from start to finish. At the end of the path turn and look back.

2. Gaze out over the plants. Breathe in, deep and slow.

3. Recognize how each tree towers above everything to provide protection. How they care for the creatures beneath. Recognize the power in this simple act and breathe out deep and slow.

4. Find one tree, leaf, or sapling that stands out. Focus on it and breathe in. Let it represent you.

5. Hold that breath for as long as you can. Feel its pressure, the thumping pulse of momentum that follows.

6. Close your eyes and visualize the pulse of the plant, the trees surrounding it, the city, the world and breathe out. See the importance of protecting others as everyone works together to live in balance.

7. Breathe in, ready to meet higher purposes, to take on whatever comes. Greet others. Smile at them like a tall tree. Encourage them in their growth, offer the protection of your humanity. This will ground the spirit.

Mountains

Thoughts manifest differently based on where a person is. When journeying the paths that lead up mountains, the air thins, forcing the body to work harder. This exertion induces an elevated mind.

Smaller mountains can be conquered in a day and do not require special equipment or much preparation, yet they still host new aspects of life. Even the smallest peaks hold new lessons. The greatest peaks on the planet are beyond the natural reach of humanity. Oxygen levels and temperatures drop so low that teams must work together to prepare and travel with the means to keep everyone alive on such an ascent.

There are plenty of mountains one can climb without risking their life. In the context of the spiritual, breaking records or proving a point is not the goal; reaching the top provides insight and a chance for reflection. It reminds us that challenges are a part of life. Even just going up an incline or a slight hill can have a similar effect if we are experiencing mobility or health issues. Working to learn the reasoning behind each hardship and influence it to better one's self can be practiced when hiking up a peak.

At higher elevations, ecosystems are less crowded. There is no room for overpopulation. The plants and animals that inhabit these areas must be instinctual and strong. Hiking trails that carry us up and up provide clarity. Even when traveling with a small group of people, there is a sense of solitude. It is easier for me to make peace with my selfish needs and work toward incorporating them into meeting the needs of the whole. A sense of oneness comes from this.

Difficult Trails

Depending on the range, planning can be as extensive as needed. Around the bottom of a mountain, the climb does not seem very strenuous. It is easy to pick up the pace, but a steady climb is more rewarding.

Taking the time to examine the trees and bushes that thin out as the path ascends displays resilience. Spotting wild goats or mountain lions is an event that hikers will never forget. It is humbling.

Taking care around steep ledges and hard drop-offs requires patience and courage, especially when we are already concentrating on focusing on our surroundings. Deep, rhythmic breathing focuses the mind and keeps a person in control of their emotions. Knowing one's own strengths and weaknesses is important here.

The main thing to focus on when climbing high altitudes is the atmosphere. Instead of thinking about tight muscles or sore feet, glancing at the trail and where it leads provides a lifeline. Beyond that passageway is the pinnacle of exploration. Once it is reached, meditation can harness the fresh accomplishment and use it as a boost of power:

1. Find a steady spot at the top and either sit or stand.

2. Scan the areas below. Look back to the trail that brought you here.

3. Breathe in and think of everything that was experienced on the way up. Breathe out and clear your mind.

4. Now with a clear head, close your eyes and hone the senses. What sounds do you notice? What does the air smell and taste like? How does it feel?

5. Visualize your body as if it were the gateway to all the messages of the world. Feel the energy build within: the thumping of your heart, the tingling of your skin.

6. It may take a while, but a flood of voices should rush in. Sort through them. Find the one that calls the loudest and answer. Be respectful, wise, and kind.

7. Let the conversation go as needed. When needed, end it and look around again. Study everything beneath the feet. Gaze up to the sky

and think of the infinite universe and how everyone fits into it. Bow and return down the trail.

Wildlife

The mountains belong to the birds. Other animals claim portions of the ranges, but it is the high fliers who truly grace the land when it's time to rest the feathers.

For centuries birds have represented peace and hope. They remind people of freedom. A free bird is truly at peace with the world. Like these winged creatures, humanity craves untethered spirits. They require wide spans to fulfill their purpose. Atop a mountain, one feels as close to the heavens as a bird soaring through the sky.

Birds hold their own magic. A power and grace resides under down and fluff. To mimic this energy certain meditations bring us closer:

1. While hiking, be aware of your habitat. Wait for a bird to fly nearby. Watch the creature.

2. Feel the energy within and extend it to that bird.

3. Visualize its perspective. Imagine the wind in its wings, and how small the world looks from up above.

4. Remember that we are just one small part of the world we inhabit. Instead of feeling inconsequential, allow any societal pressures that rest on you to fly away. Appreciate the balance of having a place in nature while many others maintain their spot as well.

5. Explore this thought with the bird as a guide. What makes you soar? How can you swoop around the difficulties you face?

Scenery

Depending on the mountain, plant life can be as diverse as any other place. In warmer areas, prickly plants and cacti paint the landscape. In cooler climates, conifers dust the span with green lace. A person could travel to different mountains and get to know the varying plants, or befriend just one area. Neither approach is better than the other. One produces a larger body of experience, but the other creates a specific one. That is up to individual goals, tastes, and spiritual links.

No matter how it is grown, the vegetation speckling a mountain signifies life and perseverance. It stands out to say, "Here I am. Thriving as I will."

Steep climbs and gradual rounds don't offer as much in-the-moment control, but they host surprises around every turn. Mountain hikes host plenty of rewards at each step, but there is less individual command. These areas don't care about our desires. They thrive on balance and the natural order. Part of that order is letting everything progress in its time.

When hiking through mountain land, its best to clear the schedule and follow the sun and moon. Forget about cramped schedules and to-do lists. Out in the open air, the world is more alive. Explore its rhythm.

Gathering the lessons learned on these hikes and bringing them back down the mountain into daily life draws more from within. Keeping what was seen and the energies felt in mind to ease our woes after returning to societal responsibility is powerful and will aid anyone on their spiritual journey.

Taking the time to appreciate and absorb the impact of the landscape along a mountain trail lends one strength. The air is cleaner. The atmosphere is calmer. The potential to improve multiplies.

To receive the full effect, meditate on a specific plant to further the connection:

1. Clear the mind and slowly soak up the surrounding view. Wait for a plant to call to you. It should draw your eye or stand out somehow.

2. Go to it and extend your hands. Place them around a stalk, bud, or branch, as close as possible without actually touching. Visualize the skin touching the energy of the plant and the air it creates as if it were able to be spotted by the naked eye.

3. Feel the power of this single growth. Let it guide you to recognize your own power. Meditate on how a person needs to be rooted in certain ways, but grow in others. What roots do you need to lie down and take hold of? What growths are ready to flourish?

Deserts/Sandy Beaches

Warm sand. Bright sunshine. Deserts and beaches are very different areas, but their magical properties are highly linked. Barefoot walks on countless granules can boost powerful energies. Despite contrasting biological makeup, the plants and animals that survive the sands are connected.

Hiking along a beach is strenuous. The resistance underfoot challenges muscles and develops character, but the water is there to spray cooling refreshment. The salt in the air cleanses the lungs. Small creatures dig their way up and scuttle along. Camouflage protects them from those who do not wait.

All of these elements come together. They encourage my spirit and its growth whether I'm visiting my favorite public lake, traveling to the Gulf of Mexico, or venturing to the sandy heat outside of Las Vegas. The energies worked within sand hold timeless power that I can easily preserve within myself if I focus enough.

Also of interest are plants growing here. Whatever washes ashore and grows along a beach places a truly unique mark on the land. I highly recommended visiting both at least once. It is well worth the effort, if only to do nothing other than sit before the waters and meditate on the air. When that is not possible, implementing a small sand garden in or around the home can offer a similar aspect. The span between them does not matter so much as the consciousness of the mysteries buried beneath.

Tough Treks

A well-cared-for body aids a well-trained mind. A well-trained mind leads to a well-defined spirit. Everything in life is connected: experiences, thoughts, actions, changes, and surprises. Combining everything to complete one's existence requires tests of strength, dedication, knowledge, and power.

A person never knows what they are capable of until they have to go as far as possible. Hiking or jogging along the shore doesn't just get the blood flowing, it creates a better opportunity to expand the mind. Likewise, driving your legs onward through endless dunes better acquaints them with the heart. It allows time to focus on goals and visualize what will occur once finished with the desert hike.

This form of meditation is for those who have practiced and grown comfortable with less-physical practices. Meditation is not just for a still body; there are other channels and pools inside us that do not wake unless in motion. A "runner's high" occurs when we reach our optimum pace. The brain relaxes and thoughts drift down new avenues. Like that journey, sand hikes induce explosive thought processes.

Following those images and ideas inside the brain leads to new awakenings. One of the best ways to do this is the following:

1. Keep a steady pace. Let your feet move in rhythm, arms swinging in time.

2. Stare ahead. Let your body follow the path while your mind clears.

3. Inhale and exhale to the beat. Hear each breath almost echo in your head.

4. The mind will sharpen but also drift. Ask yourself what this journey means at this point in life. The answers will start to come. Focus on them. Give each new idea its own time to present itself.

5. As you near the end, shift the questions to the path. Visualize its importance to others. How long has it been here? Imagine others on the same journey.

6. Thank the trail and yourself. Thank the people who came before and wish those who follow well.

Wildlife

Sandy beaches and deserts both host their own wise creatures. The ones that represent longer life spans, strength, power, and beauty are often less attainable. From feathers to shells, not even water can truly separate the divine creatures. They may face incompatible elements at times, but that does not prevent them from sharing certain qualities.

Desert birds have to be diligent. They cannot miss a detail around them. Prey is scarce and so hunting is life. But beyond that they do not need to migrate; in fact, some birds migrate to desert areas to escape cold weather. Owls and hawks who adapt to desert life are keen. They learn to listen, to watch, to be patient, all things people know to aid success in their endeavors.

Like humans, whales, dolphins, and other large marine animals have deep family connections and their own bouts of childhood playfulness that grow into maturity. The adults keep some of their fun side but with fewer unbridled acts that can lead to danger.

Our complex thought processes set us apart: sometimes they aid progress, other times they lead to complications that would otherwise be sorted out using easier, instinctual behaviors. Not all creatures inhabiting the sand are helpful guides. Some are defensive, harsh. Scorpions and tarantulas lead rough lives. They do not care about anything but survival.

There comes a time when we must grow up and accept what we have been through. It takes work and difficult reflection, but if we wish to be fully balanced people who enjoy life, we cannot just survive. The healing process cannot be rushed, nor should we feel wrong for shouldering any kind of burden. When the time comes, the way forward will make itself known.

To connect to the better part of animal kind on a sandy hike:

1. Observe the area as you go. Wait for an encounter, or visualize what life is like for the wiser creatures of the land. Step off the path.

2. See yourself as that creature, how its life feels. Think of the art of minimizing your own concerns like that animal. Instead of fearing societal issues, connect that to the baseline woes that lay beneath them: obtaining food, finding shelter, and keeping warm.

3. Let your energies intertwine with these thoughts. Trust in the instincts that guide everyone to seek out their needs and meet them. Trust in the fates that scatter through life like the sands.

4. Keep a safe distance. Bow to the animal or the idea of one if none are present. Then bury feet in granules. Sit. Close your eyes. Though part of you is buried, you have the means to pull yourself out. Meditate on this. Let your strength grow. No matter what has happened or what will be, you have the means to keep going right now.

5. Then pull feet back out and finish hike.

Plant Life

Resilience is an admirable quality. It is needed when trekking through sand. That endurance exists in many forms, but the amount of it contained in desert plants is an example of true persistence when facing adversity.

Beach grasses are tough; they don't take a beating without a fight. Seaweed and even driftwood possess a special power that humans can draw from. Despite hurricanes, typhoons, rolling tides, and even human-made atrocities like shipwrecks and oil-spills, sandy-beach plants find a way to thrive. That determination to grow leads to successes that benefit not only the plants themselves but also the ecosystem that feeds off of them. Many creatures would perish without the strength of these plants, a fact deserving of respect.

Self-exploration is the central focus of spirituality to give individuals the ability to understand who they are so they can better navigate the world. When one has control over themselves, they are fully equipped to help others and face all the realms of life. When spotting a sand plant that stands out on the trail, a simple rite can be done to connect greater ties:

1. Kneel before the plant. Meditate on it—clear your mind and focus on one aspect.

2. Reach forward, placing one hand on the soil directly in front of the plant and the other above. Close your eyes. Feel the energies within reaching for those coming from the plant. Focus on that link.

3. Think, whisper, chant, or sing a few words about finding the strength within and exuding it as the plant does.

4. Using one hand, bury the other hand under the sand. Close your eyes and visualize the wounds of the past decomposing into the grains. Dig out that hand and sit back. Lie down and play in the sand to ground yourself.

Scenery

The contrast of sky over sand is humbling. It illuminates the world when hiking over dunes. Gazing beyond the grains leades us to our imagination. What we see paints visions and images that lead us to new destinies. There is cleansing power in hiking on sand—something inside us is purified. By this power, we can recall our spirit's adventures before this life or any beyond. Time is a strange concept, one that scientists are always studying. We know it is relative, that it changes based on our perception.

Visions of timeless passages are like a dream. They require traces, most often induced by exertion of the body, ancient music, and losing grip on reality through projection or natural enhancers like absinthe, wines, and certain herbs and juices.

The approach is entirely up to the subject, but the base ritual is simple:

1. Find a secluded spot in a wide span of beachfront or desert land on a stormy day. Make sure the weather is not too hazardous, just cloudy at best. Set up music or focus on the sounds of the atmosphere.

2. Breathe in and gaze up to the uncertain sky. Exhale and look to the sand below.

3. Close your eyes and reach arms out on either side. Think of the whole of history, its predictions for the future, and for how long humanity has recorded its place here before the present day.

4. Clear your mind. To go back, recall each memory one by one, going backward. If you are searching forward, do the opposite. Start at the earliest memory and play them through the mind one by one. Start slow at first but let the pace increase as thoughts near the present. Rock or sway as needed. Let the music brought with or provided by nature meld with the memories.

5. When reaching the beginning/or the present, drop to the ground and sit. Reach further. Let the energies keep rewinding/ or fast-forwarding. Visions, words, or feelings may present themselves from eras previous to or after this one.

Cave/Cavern Exploration

Enclosed passages and rooms stand all over the globe. Some are hidden. Some peek out from rocky hillsides. They all harbor special energies and properties that aid magic.

These enclosed formations differ from every other path. Where the skies usually guide people along, stone and damp air block it all out. Hiking this kind of space opens up different senses; it hosts other elements. Caves are where the instincts cannot be silenced.

Single room caves are better for beginners. They do not all wind beneath the earth and branch off in many directions. They host large openings that can welcome newcomers. It is these rooms that provide a secluded, but not too closed off, space to block out the world and home in on personal power. That power speaks to the instincts.

By contrast, caverns are a series of openings and passages that can go on for as long as possible. It is easy to mix up the two. Caverns are caves, but not all caves are caverns. These multi-chamber rock openings are best explored by more knowledgeable hikers, and anyone venturing to these great geological formations needs to be aware that people die in caves each year.

Only perform the following practices in public caves and alert others of your intentions beforehand. Also research the area and the weather before traveling inside. If you are not comfortable with or able to do cave exploration, similar experiences can be performed in a basement or even before a rock formation in a yard, park, or familiar area.

To further extract instincts from the inner recesses of the subconscious, perform this simple rite:

1. Walk the entire curvature of the cave, brushing your fingertips along the rock wall. Feel the bumps and uneven surface beneath feet.

2. Now turn, and close your eyes.

3. Inhale and walk as in step 1, now only relying on your sense of touch and this new, limited experience. Go slow. Do not rush this process. If you stumble, catch yourself, but keep your eyes closed.

4. When you believe you've reached where you first started, stop and look back. Bow to the cave and yourself.

Finding the Way

Gaining your bearings in an earthy passage is nothing like finding your way through any other geological area. Your sense of direction is blocked by shadows and the area's makeup. Instead of choosing which way to go or an alternate route, cavern explorers are at the mercy of the underground. Hiking through a place that determines most of what we can do is an exercise in letting go. The instinct of self-preservation and the desire to control everything around us are both challenged. In these situations, we are required to grow and reach a new understanding to go further.

Journeys like this aid the spirit. They test it while also adding experiences that feed it. To bring everything together and make a cave or cavern exploration a fully connected event, use the following rite, which can be performed at any or every stage of the trip:

1. Enter the space, soaking in everything, not just the sight of the formations and creatures, but also the musty scent, the cool yet blanketed feel, the echo of moisture dripping, and footfalls.

2. Step lightly and seek out a pebble, a small single broken piece of rock. When you find one, take it in your hands.

3. Turn in the direction of the entrance and hold the pebble to chest and then kiss it. Then close your eyes and hold it to your forehead.

4. Clear your mind. Let the energies within call to the energy of the area and the pebble specifically.

5. Visualize a safe journey with many revelations. Think of that image as an entity with its own force. Now push it into the pebble.

6. Hold the pebble in your hand and turn back in the direction of the path. Rub the pebble along the way.

7. When finished, kiss it again. Either keep the pebble as a reminder of strength, or toss it back into the cave or cavern for the next person.

Wildlife

Cave dwellers add personality to an otherwise barren land. Bats are well-known for their love of cavern ceilings. Though vilified in the folklore and myths of the past, these nocturnal fliers are noble creatures. They do not often bother with humans—they have little need to.

Given the power of moonlight and the cover of darkened skies, those more in tune with their energies and the earth's magical elements enjoy this quieter time. Everything has its place, but bats are generally found huddled together when spotted by cave explorers. They sometimes shake or rustle their wings when facing a flashlight beam, but that's about it.

The pools and hidden ponds and lakes found within caverns also house cave salamanders, spiders, centipedes, millipedes, and crickets. Some people detest these creepy-crawly creatures that share our world, but these beings have their own energies and power. They represent a life without worry of the rest of the world. Unlike bats, they have no cute furry exterior to make them more palatable to society. Making use of that quality to ease our own misgivings and lessen our prejudices is a rite that can benefit even the most openhearted individuals.

Everyone has some kind of aversion or irrational fear of some living being. To determine whether this is a better instinct or just superficiality:

1. Find a cave dweller. Kneel before it and bow your head. Recall everything that induces the negative connotations harbored for it or whatever/whoever causes such a reaction.

2. Look at the creature. Try to shine some light on it, but not enough to scare it away. Study it. Get an up-close understanding of its function. Visualize its purpose. Connect that purpose to the one whom you have issue with, if not this creature.

3. Now think of your purpose. Link the two. See them as parallels. Shut off the light and meditate in the dark for a few moments.

4. Bow and then continue on.

Plant Life

Rock walls, moisture, and darkness don't breed much vegetation. These places are devoid of trees and shrubs. Yet, some plant life prefers the darkness. Like other cave dwellers, growths that spring from dirt and rock without light can be beautiful in their own way. Subtle tones and light contrasts give caverns their own atmosphere. They are a unique world.

Mosses and algae are the only plants that typically grow in underground conditions. They may not flower or produce vibrant patters, but they cleanse the air enough to support life and feed any fish or insects that inhabit the area. They make do with what is given. Instead of reaching beyond in search of light, mosses and algae thrive in places most people and creatures could not last for long periods of time. There is a strong power in this kind of survival. Drawing from that, one can benefit from the following ritual:

1. Walk up to the moss or algae. Exhale. Place hands atop it (if you need to kneel before the algae floating on a pool, do so).

2. Inhale. Visualize the skin and the plant sharing their energies.

3. Steady your breathing. Bow your head and clear your mind. Focus only on your sense of touch and meditate on it. Forget your outer shell—let the person inside come to the forefront.

4. Your hands or head may tingle. When finished, if you are willing, take a small piece of the algae or moss. Cup it in your hands and think,

whisper, chant, or sing its praises. Then eat that small bit of dark earth plant life. Get past the taste and visualize the power this food provides.

Scenery

Speaking of the scenery and visual beauty of a cave may seem like discussing how music tastes or how a warm hug sounds. The qualities that humans associate with objects, areas, or creatures are too often based on previous notions. Despite this, there are aesthetics to be found in shadowy earth tones.

Stalagmites and stalactites develop as natural sculptures. Cold, clear water sources ripple at the slightest touch. Groups of bats coat cavern ceilings with silky black fur almost like their own version of the night's sky. Mosses and algae add just enough color for diversity, while white and transparent invertebrate and blind newts display an appearance that mystifies.

Caverns and caves are not as empty as they seem when we consider their wildlife, plants, and geology. Those who take the time to explore these areas find them invigorating.

Enclosed habitats inspire in different ways. They host lesser known creative elements, making their confines the ideal location for a rite of confidence:

1. Find a space to sit or kneel before a stalagmite or stalactite. If one is not available, a large rock formation or even cave walls will do.

2. Stare at the grooves, bumps, and edges of the site. Run fingers over faces. Think of the features, pores, and flaws. Individually they may stand out as defects, but together they encompass a spirit like no other. Meditate on the whole, how even blemishes come together to create a beautiful being.

3. As energies build, stand and look at the formation from a new angle. It is the same, just as a person ages. Reach forward and place your left hand on the formation. Place your right hand on your body: run it over your shoulders, chest, and stomach. Recognize every aspect.

4. Exhale all the things you dislike about your physical appearance. Inhale the beauty of the whole. Visualize yourself as a great natural wonder.

5. Bow to the site and finish the hike.

Spells

Hiking is a meditative act that hosts plenty of room for spiritual growth. Spells performed atop a mountain or within a cave explore as much internally as outside of one's body. The following spells enhance this journey.

MOUNTAIN HIKING SPELL

Birds are mystical guides. They are intelligent enough to rise above and yet instinctual in their ways. Humanity has the tools to use intelligence along with instincts that have kept us thriving for thousands of years. Those who do so find the future less threatening than others.

To weave a spell using the avian example:

1. Hike along a mountain trail. Be diligent. Keep your senses open. Look for a feather (note that they are not always easy to find in this area). When you find one, pick it up and brush your fingertips along its edges. Visualize the air this feather must have known.

2. Let the cool cleansing idea wash over the body. Use the pointer finger of your dominant hand to draw an image representing your need on the feather. Whether you are seeking more endurance, energy, or answers, hold the feather in palm of hand once you are done, then place other hand over it.

3. Imagine the energies within at their starting point, wherever they feel most potent (usually the heart or chest). Let those energies flow out and into the feather. Think of the image you drew, what it means in practical life. See it taking hold.

4. Hold the feather above your head and let it go on the next gust of wind. If the air is stagnant, let it go when you sense the time is right.

5. Sit and press your palms against the ground. Clear your head and then get back to hiking.

CAVE EXPLORATION SPELL

If you are fully prepared, what follows is a series of tiered rituals.

1. Stand at the cave opening. Peer in without a flashlight. Clear the mind. Focus on the darkness ahead.

2. Visualize a safe passage.

3. Walk or crawl into the cavern with whatever lighting and equipment you have.

4. Go as far as needed. When the path opens up, stop and bow. Then stand or kneel and turn off the light. Again, gaze into the dark, but this time whisper or chant what it is you wish to find.

5. Listen. Do any creatures answer back?

6. Visualize them, or the cavern, answering. It may bring new thoughts to your mind.

7. Turn the light(s) back on and continue. Repeat this process as needed, each time letting the spirit of the space guide thought and energies.

8. When ending journey, stop just before exiting. Look back. Shut off light. Feel the atmosphere. Remember any answers received. Turn toward the entrance and walk through with new wisdom.

4
SWIMMING

We crave water. It is a necessity for life. Without proper hydration, we shrivel and die. Relying on such a powerful element is instinctual. Using it goes beyond health and wellness. It is a spiritual aspect of our lives that can bring forth destruction or salvation.

Hydration and proper nutrition replenish the body but these represent only a fraction of our connection to this unpredictable resource. Wading on beaches, swimming, and experiencing the wonder of remaining outside in a rainstorm speak to my being. The waters have insight to offer. They hold every truth. They have seen more than anything else on this planet. Even floating in a bath or kicking in a wading pool can provide the links necessary for many of the practices mentioned in this chapter.

Every drop on this planet has been here longer than human history; they flowed through ancient civilizations and leaders great and horrid alike to the present day. Every drop rained on the sorrows of destruction and nourished the greatest moments. Tapping into that vast energy is not something one can master in a day, week, month, or even year. It takes a lifetime of dedication.

Swimming to Survive

There are other ways to drown than in water. Life is full of obstacles that can choke the air from a person. Negative actions, reactions, thoughts, and pressures sweep through life like flash floods without warning. The saying "when it rains, it pours" doesn't even begin to contain the truth of the matter.

Learning to swim in all facets of life is an art, a practice that requires perseverance. The first step down this channel is to learn the physical side of swimming. Because floods and unexpected weather events are known to occur, learning the proper strokes and methods of keeping your head literally above water is a necessity, a life skill.

I was a born swimmer but had to learn to move with the flow as a child. Once I mastered water and its currents, I was better able to transpose what I learned into knowledge. Over time that knowledge spilled into other less obvious pools of energy and wisdom.

Everyone faces bullying or ridicule at some point. Like a rock sticking out of the middle of a stream, being treated in this negative way makes us feel divided, as if we are half a person. It slows the rush of happiness and drags on the spirit. But like water, people do not have to stop when others get in their way. An alternate flow is always possible. It's not easy—sometimes the weight of the object of pain will follow—but this is where wet elements wear down whatever blocks them.

Erosion is a long, slow process. Ignoring a bully and letting their harshness roll away is more graceful than letting it damn your progress. Depending on the extent and severity of the interactions, that may not be an option, which is where erosion becomes a tool. Don't lash out, sharp and angry. Slowly destroy the argument with intelligence and grace. Even if it does not deter the interloper, it aids the current within.

Visit a stream or river and experience the power:

1. Walk through a stream or along a river. Look to the rippling current. Find a space slowed by a log, rock, or other object.

2. Go as close to it as possible. Visualize the person(s) blocking your way as the object(s).

3. Allow all emotions toward them to surface.

4. Now, either remove the object and set it ashore, or empathize with it. It is stuck, effectively drowning itself in being an obstacle.

5. Place your palms on the surface of the water. Imagine your frustrations being washed away. Bow to the water and go on your way.

Swimming Together

Self-imposed pressures are an internal struggle best handled with meditation, hiking, and swimming. I am never satisfied with my accomplishments; there is always something else to be done or another branch of an idea to be explored. It is mentally exhausting. To balance this, physical activity aids my brain and frees the spirit. Reveling in my own power reminds my subconscious of the strength hiding deeper.

The instinct to criticize ourselves exists to maintain positive outcomes, but can stunt personal growth in the modern age. Images of others and their accomplishments are plastered all around. Comparisons are only natural. Again, here water is a perfect guide. Streams and rivers do not care what the other bodies of water are doing. They continue on their way and connect with other sources to reach greater spaces.

That example is a perfect representation of positive energy. As much as people feel the need to compete with each other, there is also an instinct to come together and do greater things with the support of a group, community, or population. For help in reaching this communal mindset:

1. Visit a lake or stream in spring, summer, or fall. Walk gently along the water's edge seeking out minnows or tadpoles with a small bucket.

2. When you find some, kneel down and study how they move about. Each individual has their own purpose, but the school or group works together to warn each other of danger.

3. Use the bucket to scoop up one or a few of these small creatures. Kneel before it and dip fingertips into water. Watch the animal's reaction. Study its movements.

4. Visualize yourself as that small tadpole or fish. Let the energies within build and pour them into the water.

5. Release whatever you caught into the water, watching it swim back to the others. Observe the slight difference they all hold.

6. Meditate on the idea of community. Think of balancing who you are with the desires and needs of your family, friends, community, and beyond. When done, wade in the water barefoot as a form of grounding.

Keeping Afloat–No Drowning

Air is life. When it fills the lungs, the body floats and allows a person be safe in water. When panicking, people tend to gasp and flail. This expels more air than it takes in, and leads the body to sink underwater. This reaction is just a reflex—we cannot control our anxiety and panic in times of peril unless we have a higher connection to our energies.

Breathing helps but is not enough to protect ourselves from drowning. There has to be movement, a fight to live and the will to succeed. Applying this philosophy in everyday life creates a clear path.

The spirit cannot be broken no matter what it faces if it flows as free as the waters that nourish it. Gaining that strength comes from rites such as the following:

1. Fill your bathtub and lock yourself in the bathroom. Tune out the world.

2. Light candles or add floral oils to create a calming atmosphere.

3. Step into the tub and sit. Cup water in hands. Stare at the image looking back. See the worry, the concern. Splash the water on your face. Visualize it washing the anxiety from your features.

4. Do the same for the shoulders, arms, chest, and back. Think of all that makes you sink further down in despair.

5. Lie down and completely submerge your body. Hold breath for as long as possible. Let the water absorb the anxiety and depression. Let the cleansing power heal hidden wounds.

6. Come up for air and breathe deep. Inhale solutions. Exhale the fears. With each breath remember the worst struggles you have survived and how they were resolved. The answers will come in time.

True Freedom

To balance the body in a situation we have little to no control over, water is a perfect answer. I came from an unstable home life. Swimming was my sanctuary. In summertime, the waters washed away the pains my father caused and helped me to forgive my mother for allowing him to continue hurting us.

Always a cleansing source, water doesn't just purify the skin, organs, and blood—it also reduces or blocks out frequencies depending on the depth. Going for a swim underwater or lying in a shallow pool offers a slight reprieve to help the body cope with all it experiences. Solitude is a part of humanity's instinctual needs. Even just a few minutes alone every once in a while aids one in knowing who they are and finding the power within.

In essence, water not only provides the space to do this but gives individuals the freedoms they seek as well. No matter how social a person is, everyone needs time to be in their own head. Underwater thoughts drift in waves of continuous synchronicity. They hydrate instincts. A fuller, healthier mind emerges from the depths of clear, cool ritual.

To filter out unwanted messages and reclaim the body and brain as a single entity, try the following:

1. Go to a pool of any kind. (Natural water sources are best, but even a public pool can help.)

2. Walk into it waist-deep. Look up to the sky. Visualize all the transmissions being sent in that span above and around everyone. Imagine how many messages, words, hopes, dreams, horrors, painful omissions, and disappointments are out there.

3. Think of how these touch the body and go through it. See how we swim in what carries our mental transmissions.

4. Now clear the mind. Block everything out and leave it behind. Take a deep breath and sit underwater. Paddle hands underwater to remain sitting.

5. Feel the difference. Let the body relax. Stay beneath the chaos and unwanted frequencies rushing through us to deliver their messages.

6. Feel the release, the freedom—true freedom. It is freedom of thought. The power to use our own singular, untainted thoughts is true individual peace.

7. Come up for air. The body should remain relaxed.

8. If willing, walk further in, up to the chin and repeat. Do this going deeper and deeper as needed until the world comes into focus.

9. For anyone keen on scuba diving, even with all the equipment and gear, diving below human capability takes us further away from the land of crowded thought and overpopulated airways. This is best done without underwater computers and gadgets, as they produce their own condensed energies.

10. When you are finally finished, sit with just your feet in the water. Meditate on the stillness beneath the surface. Keep that stillness. Remember it until it is time to return.

Trust in Fate

When blocking out the excess, water serves as not only a filter but also a gateway. Like humanity, water is made up of a giant population of individual drops that have the power to sway the world alone but have much more influence when strengthened in large numbers that rush together.

When meditating, I call upon my own inner light; a great warmth floods my body. Even in darkness, this rush of comfort is available. It is as if Poseidon or lesser known aquatic deities are attracted to that instinctual power. Other times, it is the water creatures who bring divinity with their presence. Swimming in shallows can call on smaller entities. When learning to scuba dive, I found myself so exhilarated when a circle of fish surrounded me. The other divers and even our instructor stopped to watch in awe. "Looks like someone's part water," our instructor said. I have always joked that I am part mermaid, but there is something to be said about the need to swim and extend energies to the waters of the earth. It was as if the fish had come to protect me out of respect or attraction to my energies. It was incredibly comforting.

When even the most shunned and vulnerable creatures come to you with love and trust, you have reached a special point in existence. This pertains to water especially when swimming. Water bugs and flying insects love to skim the water. Fish surface and jump when the coast is clear. Water snakes slither atop water as if they could walk. When these particular creatures come toward us, it can be jarring. Floating along a calm current to roll over and meet a serpentine gaze face-to-face makes the heart pound, but it too is a sign of respect. It is proof of a deeper connection to the world.

When meeting these entities or animals, there is a rite that can be done to ease the shock and veer the moment into its proper place:

1. Do not move (whether under water or at the surface). Out of respect for the entity or creature, remain still.

2. Observe its presence. Some creatures swim around and keep going, others stick around to study us as much as we look over them.

3. Bow to the being, or the water left behind it.

4. Clear the mind and send out positive energies.

5. Soak up the feeling surrounding the body. Use that emotion or sensation to react or respond if you feel compelled to do so. If the creature reacts, move slowly and gracefully.

6. When the creature has left, meditate on what happened.

Ritual Baths

Baths have become less common due to the popularity of modern showers, but they still serve a purpose. Running water to sit in is less rushed. Instead of getting in and out after a quick scrub, soaking in the waters one has drawn recalls the knowledge our ancestors sought in the past. Meditations and adventuring through the wilderness offer plenty of perspective, but the body needs recuperation. The skin gets marred and covered on long explorations.

Rituals to use bathing for personal power vary. Some are meant to cleanse the body before performing rites. Spells are more expansive. When weaving energies to create specific outcomes, purification is not the objective but the starting point to build from. The waters will cool as needed.

Taking the time to prepare for ritual and spellwork is an art form. It draws out the best of the spirit. Like a child who carries their favorite bath toys into the tub, these little ceremonies are less about how luxuriously appointed the bath may be and more about what the items mean to us personally. Anyone can buy a flower; it takes more effort to grow one and let its beauty live on.

The body may be cleansed in any old shower or bath; it is the spirit, our energies, and the power that connects us to the universe that are touched by these practices. Ritual baths, bathing spells, and the fun of whimsical memories are easily implemented in homes no matter how civilization changes.

Purification

The elements around us are all instruments. They can be played beautifully to harmonize with the spirit or ignored. Water, in this instance, is a difficult source to be left behind. It lingers inside the body. It is always working to aid us. With a purified mind, finding the strength and courage to face the world with an open heart is made possible no matter what one has suffered.

Ritual baths are often the start to a fresh body:

1. Make the preparation part of the rite. Scrub the tub clean, make sure the bathroom space is as welcoming as possible.

2. Keep it simple. This is about cleansing the body. A light salt can be added as a neutralizer but all that is required is the tub, water, and body.

3. Fill the tub, watching the water rush into it. When ready to go in, skim the surface with hands first. Then step in slowly.

4. Lower yourself into the tub and sit. Lean back and lie down. Close your eyes. Give the body time to soak. Clear the mind.

5. Lower your head under water. Run your fingers through your hair and visualize your body radiating light and energy.

6. Resurface and slowly wash body. While rubbing each limb and area, visualize powerful rulers alongside the impoverished all doing the same as they have done before and will do after. Think of how the simple act of cleaning the body is a shared goal that is not always available to everyone.

7. Breathe in and think of everything you like about your body. Breathe out and expel all the criticisms you have of your appearance.

8. Lie back and meditate on appreciating who you are.

Healing Waters

Baths are seen as more ritualistic, but showering under a waterfall or in a bathroom hosts a different source of strength. If we are versed enough, shower energies can provide us the purification and change needed to perform a proper spell or banish unwanted elements from our life.

Showers relieve pains in the mind and the body. The repetitive drops of water hitting the floor create a rhythm that soothes the spirit. I do not have a lot of time for baths; showers are a simple source of purification, healing, and enlightenment that connects all aspects of my being and revives my senses when I've been ailing.

Shower Energies

Pacing is everything. Baths require time and care, a slow fill. Showers are seen as a convenience of modern living. People often rush in and out of the water to keep up with their busy schedules, but rushing water need not be the premise for hurried habits. The pressure of water beating down relaxes muscles. The thump of a continuous gush creates a calming rhythm. Witnessing the power of fluidity brings peace.

Whether hiking to a waterfall or showering at home, absorbing hydration from a shower increases the healing power of this element. To sooth the body, a quick showering meditation can revive personal energies:

1. Stretch one hand under the shower, palm up. This represents the power to heal. Hold your other hand out in opposite direction facing downward. This represents the injury.

2. Slowly walk into the water. Centrally stand under the water, facing the spout. Close your eyes and visualize your issue(s) in your mind's eye.

3. Hold both hands up to water source. Now imagine the cleaning power of the water growing and being absorbed into your skin. Think of it as a glowing light. Wipe your face with it. Place your hands over the affected area (or areas, one by one) and let the light aid the body in its healing process.

4. Open your eyes and bow your head. Let the water rush over back and shoulders. Think of it as medicine. Then step out.

Swimming Powers

Swimming in pools large enough to let us sink beneath the surface of the water provides an unparalleled dynamic. Complete submersion heals from all angles. It holds the power to block out harmful elements, thoughts, or energies that slow progress and overall health.

The underwater world is a realm of its own. Instead of focusing on all of the problems plaguing my life, everything slows and I find peace. It better connects my energies so I can focus on balance. When in tune with myself, I can navigate the higher power of this force and direct its better aspects.

Even floating along the ripples and bubbles atop the water is a helpful meditation:

1. Clear your mind. Breathe deep and walk waist-deep into the water.

2. Focus your energies on healing the body. Meditate on this idea; let it grow. Imagine the source of your power extending through your hands. Gently rub the affected area.

3. Walk as deeply as is comfortable, then lie flat on your back. Gaze into the sky. Breathe in and visualize the body repairing itself. Breathe out and will the pain or discomfort to subside. Repeat this breathing pattern.

4. Now close your eyes and allow the water to sooth the body. Think of the current, ripples, or bubbles as medicine being absorbed through the spine and dispersed to the injury or ailment.

5. Breathe deep once more. Regain footing and bow to the water. Then turn toward land.

6. Lie on beach to ground yourself back in reality.

Swimming in the Air

Water powers are not limited to pools and tubs. Precipitation is also magical. It holds various properties that awaken hidden qualities buried within humanity.

Shifting weather patterns, storm cycles, and pressure changes are electric. Their energies are linked to the currents we all host. Harnessing that power fine-tunes one's inner callings while reaching out to encompass the entirety of the natural world.

To "swim in the air" is to deepen broader connections through the waters that fall on land. That frame of reference goes beyond what has been taught. It taps into the understandings that everyone is born with. It brings those truths to the forefront and aids individuals to understand and know certain facts without having to study them.

Rain, snow, sleet, and hail are all charged with the purity and healing energy of every water, but in addition, these unpredictable occurrences offer the perfect atmosphere for reflection, change, and growth:

1. Go to the outdoor space as the precipitation starts. Hold out your bare hands palms up.

2. Look up and close your eyes. Feel the force of the water beating on your skin.

3. Look down. Open your eyes. Watch the water accumulate or puddle around your feet.

4. Now press your hands together. Whisper, chant, or sing about connecting your spiritual self with the water falling around you. Think

of the animals and creatures that weather this kind of storm without modern technology.

5. Now rub your wet hands on your face. Close your eyes and meditate on the sound of the precipitation, the smell in the air, the feel of the icy drops.

6. When the energies are spent, go home and drink a warm beverage to ground yourself.

Spells

Water spells are highly sacred. Because it combines the power of bathing, showering, and swimming, and the act of worshiping elements of the self in relation to the magic surrounding everyone, this breed of spell requires extended respect. Like meditations, these spells are meant to aid with issues of harm from both in- and outside the body: fertility, abuse, assault, self-harm, and confidence problems may be dealt with through bathing spells.

PURIFICATION OF THE MIND BATH

Baths to purify the body, thoughts, and spirit all exist to aid us as we grow and change throughout life. While very similar to baths for the body, baths for the mind require more aesthetic elements. The mind reacts a great deal to aromas and the feel of textures. For this reason, it is advised that you clip buds and/or pluck flower petals and leaves from a household plant or your garden to aid in cleansing thoughts. To purify your thoughts:

1. Make the preparation part of the rite. Scrub the tub clean, make sure the bathroom space is as welcoming as possible.

2. Fill the tub, watching the water rush into it. Sprinkle the flowers and leaves in a little at a time, thinking of what their beauty and presence have meant to you.

3. When ready to enter, skim the surface with your hands first, swirling the plant clippings around. Step in slowly.

4. Lower yourself into the tub and sit. Lean back and lie down. Close your eyes and give the body time to soak. Clear the mind.

5. Breathe in the earth fragrances. Let the scents lighten the feel. Cup a few clippings in your hands and watch them dance along the smaller span of your fingers and palms.

6. Slowly bring your hands up and pour the contents over your head. Think of moving forward in life. Look back on issues that still plague your mind. Wash them away, one handful of water at a time as you focus on the plants that sprung from your efforts.

7. Breathe in and think of everything you have accomplished. Breathe out and expel all the obstacles still lingering in your mind.

8. Lie back and meditate on the plants in the water. Think of how they float along even after being cut.

PURIFICATION OF THE SPIRIT BATH

After mastering purifying the body for rituals and keeping the mind cleansed, we turn to the spirit, also in need of its occasional redemption and renewal. Even the strongest wills get broken. Recharging and rebuilding is a part of life. No one can be at their best all the time, which is why a spiritual purification bath is needed:

1. Make the preparation part of the rite. Scrub the tub clean and make sure the bathroom space is as welcoming as possible.

2. Fill the tub, watching the water rush into it. Place candles around the tub. Even just one is enough to perform this act, but many are also welcome.

3. When ready to go in, light the candles and skim the surface of the water with your hands. Step in slowly.

4. Lower yourself into the tub and sit. Lean back and lie down. Close your eyes and give the body time to soak. Clear the mind.

5. Feel the warmth of the water and also the candles burning by you. Focus on one of them. Watch the flame melt the wax.

6. Visualize the flame as yourself. Imagine it melting the obstacles from your path as well as the negative energies that come with them. Banish hatred, anger, pettiness, and thoughts of revenge or retribution.

Instead, think of your life burning like the flame. It does not stop. It will not remember the wax.

7. Breathe in and focus on the oxygen feeding the light inside of you—not just your body but the spirit that is connected to your instincts and the world around you. Breathe out and feel bad for the candle's demise. Learn to pity those who try to harm others while valuing the nature of not allowing that pity to put out your spark.

8. Lie back and meditate on the light. Imagine it inside and how it manifests in how you live and what you do. When you are ready, put out the candles by submerging them in the tub with you. For all our fire, the coolness of the water is still humbling.

FERTILITY BATH SPELL

MATERIALS NEEDED: Tub, water, and self

To PREPARE: In this era, people spend so much time trying not to get pregnant that if/when the time finally comes to have a family, things do not always progress as planned. Please try for at least a year before resorting to spellwork. The body progresses at its own rates. Perform the day before *and* the day after attempted conception.

THE WORK:

1. Make sure the tub is cleaned beforehand. Then fill with water—no oils, salts, or soaps are necessary. This is a natural rite.

2. As the water rises visualize the womb filling, or the sperm being as potent.

3. Stir the water with both hands before stepping in. Sit and lie back.

4. Breathe in as deeply as possible and place your hands over your womb or under your testes. Breathe out as slowly as possible, letting go of all the pressure and anxiety that comes with hoping to start or expand a family.

5. Breathe in and focus your energies on your reproductive organs. Close your eyes and imagine your energy moving down (if it is not already in that area). Focus the mind on strengthening the ties between your body and your will to create life.

6. Meditate on a successful conception, pregnancy, and birth. Visualize the joys and pains. Accept them all.

7. Relax and let your hands float. Take a hundred deep breaths, as slow and steady as possible. Then wash body and drain tub.

WHIMSY—CHILDREN IN THE TUB, THE FUN

To quench the thirst for deeper love and stronger bonds, one must remember to laugh and love like a child. Imagine splashing in the waters of carelessness. Water is a source of reconnection to ourselves when our soul feels dried out, and there is a fun bath rite that adults can engage in if they struggle to cast aside the woes of knowledge and the expectations of the world around them.

1. Make or obtain a small toy boat meant for water play.

2. Meditate on it while filling the tub. Visualize how you would have played with it (or turned your nose up at it for whatever reason) when you were young. Feel the energy of the laughter or other reactions. Now think of young friends and cousins who shared their youth with you. Remember your best friend. Imagine your children, nieces, nephews, neighbor's kids, or friend's kids laughing and playing with a toy boat at the pool.

3. Get into the water when the tub is full. Sit up and set the boat in the water. Push it. Swirl the water around it. Knock it over and splash. Let go of worrying about others' reactions.

4. Now lie back and close your eyes. Imagine the boat sailing over your body. Visualize yourself as a hidden continent lying beneath the ocean.

5. Everything beneath the surface matters, but does not have to come ashore. Think about how all other matters disappear from the brain when you enjoy yourself. The key to enjoying life is not to always do things you like; it is learning to enjoy everything, even the actions and things that seem menial.

6. Think of how you can make the mundane fun. Imagine what can be added to a work station, car ride, or bus trip. The little things that remind us of the children we once were still draw out the best in us.

7. Sit up and grasp the boat with both hands. Let it represent your uniqueness. Let it serve as a reminder to hold on to who you were when you were young as you grow and change through life.

8. Drain the tub and dry off. Place the boat where it will be seen and remembered as a symbol of a youthful energy.

BATHTUB SPELL TO BANISH ABUSE

MATERIALS NEEDED: Tub, water, self, washcloth

TO PREPARE: Get to a safe place. If you are living in an unsafe situation, go stay with a friend, family member, or at a shelter. It does not have to be permanent, just a place to think clearly and take things a little at a time. There will be moments of weakness, but this spell will aid you in refraining from returning to a dangerous situation and will give the abuser a push toward getting themselves the mental help they need.

THE WORK:

1. Kneel before the tub and let everything resurface. Reflect on all the pain, all the moments that broke you down. Everything that led to this moment.

2. Turn on the water and cry, scream, or bite into your washcloth—whatever releases those emotions out into the world. Don't hide them or hold anything in any longer. Give yourself time to grieve and mourn.

3. Now get into the tub. Sit, lie down, or kneel; get into the most comfortable position. Hold up the washcloth and visualize your abuser's energy, their spirit radiating from the material. (If it helps, imagine them as the washcloth, a small wet rag.)

4. Plunge the washcloth into the water around you. Swirl it all around. Think of the waters rushing through this person, thinning their potency, diluting their attacks and negativity.

5. Take up the washcloth and wring it out. As the water drips down, imagine all the horrid actions or words slipping from them, leaving them naked and afraid. What led them to this behavior? Seek understanding. Were they themselves abused or traumatized? Are they abusing substances, internally stunted, or mentally ill?

6. Recognize that it is not your purpose to fix them. Hold the cloth and take pity, but then drop it where it may land and take pity on yourself for what has taken place.

7. Sink beneath the water and let the waters drown your pain. When resurfacing breathe in fresh thoughts. Look to the future. Focus on the things that inspire creativity and happiness.

8. Wash your body and cleanse your mind of all pity. Look forward to being a survivor who may offer others guidance.

9. Step out of the tub and pull the plug. While drying yourself, watch the washcloth spin and sink. Imagine them finding their way, getting help. When the water has drained, take up the washcloth and wring it out once more. Wish the abuser a new start without the desire to harm.

10. Look to the mirror and bow to the strength in yourself.

SPELL TO RECOVER FROM ASSAULT/ABUSE

MATERIALS NEEDED: Tub, water, self, and sea sponge (no substitutes—it must be from the sea)

TO PREPARE: Rest. Take the time needed to mourn your loss and what occurred. Trauma is a sort of death, but rebirth is the beauty of survival.

THE WORK:

1. Kneel before the tub and think of healing. Visualize how far you have come since getting away from the abuse. Even just a few days of personal rest and relaxation provides some progress.

2. Turn on the water and grab the sponge with both hands. Think of the pain that still affects you: bruising, scratches, raw skin, nightmares, fear of strangers, fear for the future, concerns of the abuser, and more. Cry or release the pain as needed, but push all that energy into the sponge. Focus on moving forward instead of remaining stagnant.

3. Get into the tub. Kneel, sit, or lie down; get as comfortable as possible.

4. Take the sponge and cleanse it in the healing waters of your bath. Let all the pain seep out. Think of yourself as the sponge. You absorbed so much for so long. Now it is time to wash everything away and begin anew.

5. Scrub any physical marks slowly and gently. Visualize the abusive powers of the one who harmed you being wiped away and drowned in the waters.

6. Meditate on the energies inside. Visualize them as a glowing light wherever they originate. Let them grow and spread throughout the body like armor. Feel your body become charged with power.

7. Sink beneath the water and push that energy out. Let it keep going as far as imaginable, even reaching through the person who harmed you.

8. Now relax and resurface. Pour positive energy into the sponge and wash yourself with it again. Envision yourself moving on with success and happiness. Look to new goals and activities. Do not hide from your pain, but wipe it out with each aspiration.

9. Repeat as needed.

ENDING SELF-HARM

MATERIALS NEEDED: Tub, water, self, and a flower (of any variety, best done with your favorite; make sure all thorns have been removed)

TO PREPARE: Have a conversation with yourself in the mirror. Why are you doing what you do? Explore the issue and contemplate a new mindset.

THE WORK: This is helpful for addicts, anorexics, bulimics, those who cut or burn themselves on purpose: any form of harm inflicted on one's self, by themselves.

1. Stand before tub and examine your body. Look over the areas most affected by your actions.

2. Turn on the faucet. As the water rushes into the tub, think of everything you are doing that prevents your body from being at full health. Whether a coping mechanism, an act against pressures and abuse, an addiction, or a mental issue beyond these listed, looking to this spell is a start to regaining health. Imagine the waters before you as the blood within. Rushing, churning, working to power and cleanse.

3. Now imagine the tub as a body. A vessel made of different elements that come together in one entity.

4. Get into the tub and lie down. Close your eyes. Think of a time before you hurt yourself. If no memory is found, imagine what it would have been like.

5. Take up the flower and just brush the petals in the water. Anoint them with health and life. See them coming together to make up one beautiful flower. Now roll the flower over the areas most affected by actions. For example: hips and ribs for anorexics; throat and stomach for bulimics; cuts or scabs for skin mars, the mouth, anus, or other entry sites for addicts.

6. Kiss the flower and rest with it, lying across your chest. Hold it close. Let it purify and bless you inside and out.

7. Visualize yourself as the flower. Delicate and mortal, accept that pain is a part of life, but feel the balance. Harming yourself does nothing to aid with personal growth or spiritual power. It holds us back. Any returns that come from self-harm are dark and degrading.

8. Vow to love the body you were born into and care for it as you would a flower.

9. Let the flower go and see it float with grace and truth. Bow to this dignity. Place hands atop surface of the water and absorb that energy.

10. When ready, pull the plug and set flower on the edge of the tub. Leave it for at least a day as a symbol of the beauty within and how that shines outward when we fulfill our true nature.

BATHING CONFIDENCE SPELL

MATERIALS NEEDED: Tub, water, self, and a song to sing

TO PREPARE: If you feel you are too shy to sing aloud, make sure you're home alone.

THE WORK:

1. Fill the tub with water and enter the bath. Sit up and think of all the criticism you have for yourself inside and out.

2. Lie back and think of at least three things you love about your body, three about your mind, and three about your spirit. Touch your chest and start singing the song. Touch the head on the next phrase. Then clasp your hands on the next phrase. Let the song recall more positive attributes.

3. When the song is over, sink beneath the water. Visualize all the attractive, seemingly happy people out there. Think of all the plain individuals who have found success and happiness. No matter who they are or what they look like, how they act and feel is the main energy that increases power.

4. Search for that power inside yourself. Find it. Hold on to it. Focus on the best of who you are and resurface.

5. Now sit forward and sing the song again, louder, surer. Let the music stay with you.

SHOWERING TO EASE MENTAL ISSUES

MATERIALS NEEDED: Shower and self

TO PREPARE: No preparation needed.

THE WORK:

1. Step into the shower. Turn to face away from the spout. Rub your hands all over your body, slowly at first then picking up the pace to build energy.

2. Now grasp your left wrist with your right hand, and your right wrist with your left hand. Bow your head and exhale all the toxins plaguing your mind. Gaze upward and breathe in clarity and focus. Repeat these breaths at least ten times, if not more.

3. With each breath, the body may tingle. The head may grow light. Converse with yourself and any energies that may present themselves. Let the water guide you to repeat as needed to heal and strengthen the mind.

SHOWERING TO HEAL SPIRITUAL WOES

MATERIALS NEEDED: Shower and self

TO PREPARE: No preparation necessary.

THE WORK:

1. Step into the water. Turn to face away from the spout and close your eyes. Look up and let the drops rain down on your face.

2. Look down and open eyes. Stare at your feet. Watch the water run to them. Wiggle your toes and envision your body soaking up the healing power of each drop with the tips of each toe.

3. Visualize that energy growing though the bottoms and tops of your feet, through the ankles, and up your legs. Reach toward the water and visualize the same thing with your fingertips, hands, arms, and beyond until the entire body has been covered.

4. Now bend forward and touch the toes. Take a deep breath and slowly roll up, then raise your arms above your head as high as possible.

5. Close your eyes and feel the rush of energy growing. Pour it into that part of you that is spiritually pained. Let it mingle with the pain, emptiness, or negativity. Keep your arms raised until your body tingles or the energies cease.

6. Slowly lower your arms, turn, and bow to the water.

FLOATING SPELL TO MEND THE MIND

MATERIALS NEEDED: Pool of water and self

TO PREPARE: Find a body of water (preferably natural) with extra space where you can float with your arms spread wide.

THE WORK:

1. Clear your mind. Breathe deep and walk waist-deep into the water.

2. Recall recent negative thoughts. Think of the source. Where did these ideas come from? Why do they continue to weigh on you?

3. Walk as deep as comfortable, then float flat on your back. Breathe in and gaze at the sky above. Imagine all the thoughts that live in that span. Breathe out and push away the negativity.

4. Keep breathing deep. Focus on any positive outcomes, decisions, or actions that could be derived from the negative thoughts. Be creative, dig deep. Turn the bad into good with focus and control. (If you are recognizing thoughts about harming yourself or others, this can be turned around by contemplating whom to go to for help. A trusted friend, family member, or professional will understand and get the process of healing started.)

5. Now close your eyes and float along, visualizing the positivity that was born from a plague of the mind. Think of the rushing water as a pool of knowledge rushing ashore to teach its lessons. Absorb the wisdom of connection through your spine and send it up to your brain.

6. Breathe deeply once more. Regain your footing and bow to the water. Turn toward land.

7. Lie on beach to ground yourself in reality.

FLOATING SPELL TO SOOTHE THE SPIRIT

MATERIALS NEEDED: Pool of water and self

TO PREPARE: Find a body of water (preferably natural) with extra space where you can float with your arms spread wide.

THE WORK:

1. Clear your mind. Breathe deep and walk into the water as deep as is comfortable. Lie flat on your back and gaze into the sky. Visualize your body as the air that brushes against the water, how it moves as it needs and doesn't need to be seen or recognized in order to fulfill its purpose.

2. Breathe in and close your eyes. Clear your mind. Let your physical body drift away from you. Breathe out and charge your spirit with the rush of the water, the flow below.

3. Keep breathing deep. Feel the power of your life source and your connection to the energies everywhere. Focus that power on expanding the spirit's reach.

4. Float along. Visualize the depths of the water and the lands it touches. Think of the creatures that cannot live without it. Absorb the potency of nourishing the self and others; take in that wisdom from the waters through the skin.

5. Breathe deep once more. Regain your footing and bow to the water. Then turn toward land.

6. Lie on the beach to ground yourself in reality.

STROKES TO HEAL THE BODY

MATERIALS NEEDED: Body of water and self

TO PREPARE: Find a body of water (preferably natural) where you can do laps with plenty of space. This is best done for recurring issues or chronic ailments such as joint pain or arthritis.

THE WORK:

1. Walk waist-deep into the water. Skim your hands atop the water at your sides. Swirl the hands and clear the mind.

2. Breathe deep and dive forward to begin the stroke, kicking and pushing the arms as needed. As the body warms up, feel the resistance. Focus on any aches that occur.

3. Go as far as possible through the pain. When reaching an end or space to turn back, stop and look at how far you've come. Think of the pressure in the body and how it has stunted your pacing and progress.

4. Close your eyes and breathe deep. Dive and go back the way you came, only this time focus on the water. Instead of seeing it as something the body cuts through, envision it as medicine. With each stroke, the water further engages each joint, muscle, tendon, and bone.

5. Absorb the healing energy as you fight to remain active. Be conscious of your body and know your limits. After going as far as possible, stop and meditate on your physicality.

6. There should be a lightness. Your body may tingle or float easier. Splash water on your face and smile at the clear pool of water. Thank it for understanding.

7. Lie on beach to ground yourself in reality.

STROKES TO MEND THE MIND

MATERIALS NEEDED: Body of water and self

TO PREPARE: Find a body of water (preferably natural) where you can do laps with plenty of space.

THE WORK:

1. Walk waist-deep into the water. Skim your hands atop the water at your sides. Swirl your hands and clear the mind.

2. Breathe deep and dive forward to begin the stroke, kicking and pushing the arms as needed. As the body warms up, feel the resistance. Visualize that weight as the obstacles that press on your mind.

3. Go as far as possible, thinking over each recurring negative thought. When reaching the end or space to turn back, stop and look at how far you've come. Let that distance represent the positive achievements you've reached despite negative setbacks in life.

4. Close your eyes and breathe deep. Dive back to swim the way you came, only this time focus on out-swimming the negativity. With each stroke you are that much further from detrimental thoughts.

5. Feel the water splash against your face as you fight to keep going. Be conscious of the power inside of your brain. When going as far as possible, stop and meditate on strengthening the mind.

6. Some lightheadedness may occur. The body may tingle or shiver. Splash water over your head and smile at the clear water. Thank it for understanding.

7. Lie on beach to ground yourself in reality.

STROKES TO SOOTHE THE SPIRIT

MATERIALS NEEDED: Body of water and self

TO PREPARE: Find a body of water (preferably natural) where you can do laps with plenty of space.

THE WORK:

1. Walk into the water waist-deep. Skim your hands atop the water at your sides. Swirl your hands and clear your mind.

2. Breathe deep and dive forward to begin the stroke, kicking and pushing the arms as needed. As your body warms up, be conscious of the water. Visualize the churning surface as it trails around and behind whatever comes its way

3. Go as far as possible, thinking over how the soul is most charged when understanding is found. Reaching the end or space to turn back, stop and take in how still the water becomes once more. It goes back to its original form after whatever has disturbed it is gone. Meditate on how water continues to go its course no matter what interferes.

4. Close your eyes and breathe deep. Dive once again to swim the way you came, only this time focus on persisting around whatever weakens the spirit. With each stroke become one with the power of the water.

5. When reaching the end of your destination, stop and meditate on your place in the world and beyond.

6. Some lightheadedness may occur. The body may tingle or shiver. Splash water over your head and smile at the clear water. Thank it for understanding.

7. Lie on beach to ground yourself in reality.

SINKING SPELL TO HEAL THE BODY

MATERIALS NEEDED: Body of water and self

TO PREPARE: Find a body of water (preferably natural) where you can sink to a safe but appreciable depth. Good for any injury or chronic ailments.

THE WORK:
1. Swim to the deeper area (but make sure you have a feel for things such as any currents, the water's depth). Tread water.

2. Spin in a circle. Spin in the other direction. Breathe deep and dive down to the floor at a steady pace.

3. Visualize the injury or chronic ailment. Feel it affecting the body. Focus on the sensations it causes, pain, pressure, etc.

4. Hover above the sand or muddy bottom. Grab a handful of watery earth. Envision its power. Now extend the power to it and press the earth to the area of your body in need. Pour the energies into healing it from the inside out.

5. Swim to the surface at a steady pace. Breathe in deep. Look to the skies. Spin in a circle; now spin the other way. Dip your head below the surface for one second and nod to the water.

6. Lie out on beach to ground yourself in reality.

SINKING SPELL TO MEND THE MIND

MATERIALS NEEDED: Body of water and self

TO PREPARE: Find a body of water (preferably natural) where you can sink to a safe but appreciable depth.

THE WORK:

1. Swim to the deeper area (but make sure you have a feel for it, the currents, how far the bottom is). Tread water.

2. Spin in a circle. Spin in the other direction. Breathe deep and dive down to the floor at a steady pace.

3. Think of the issues that have returned to your mind, how they drown out positive ideas and energies when paired with anxiety, depression, pain, or judgment.

4. Sit above the sand or the muddy bottom. Move your hands to stay below. Imagine yourself as the water and the negative thoughts sinking beneath you and sinking into the bottom of the water's floor. Imagine burying them under new ideas and creative powers that hold promise.

5. Swim to the surface at a steady pace. Breathe in deep. Look to the skies. Spin in a circle; now spin the other way. Dip head below the surface for one second and nod to the water.

6. Lie on beach to ground yourself in reality.

SINKING SPELL TO SOOTHE THE SPIRIT

MATERIALS NEEDED: Body of water and self

TO PREPARE: Find a body of water (preferably natural) where you can sink to a safe but appreciable depth.

THE WORK:

1. Swim to the deeper area (but make sure you have a feel for it, the currents, how far the bottom is). Tread water.

2. Spin in a circle. Spin in the other direction. Breathe deep and dive down to the floor at a steady pace.

3. Leave behind selfish concerns while holding on to the main instinct of self-preservation. Visualize your energies combining with the power of the water the deeper you go. Let them hydrate the soul and your connection to existence.

4. Hover above the sand or muddy bottom. Grab a handful of the watery earth. Envision its energy reaching out for yours. Rub the mud or sand between your palms, mixing the powers and absorbing them at the same time. Open your hands and let the earth wash away.

5. Swim to the surface at a steady pace. Breathe in deep. Look to the skies. Spin in a circle; now spin the other way. Dip your head below the surface for one second and nod to the water.

6. Lie on the beach to ground yourself in reality.

RAIN SPELL TO CALL ON INSTINCTS

MATERIALS NEEDED: Rainy day, small outdoor space, medium bowl, self

TO PREPARE: Rest. Let the misty day roll through you like a fog. Wear appropriate clothing. A jacket or coat may be necessary.

THE WORK:

1. Go to outdoor space during a rainstorm. Place bowl on the ground at feet and let it collect the rain.

2. Reach up to the sky. Breathe in the electricity. Feel the water cleaning everything.

3. Reach to the ground. Breathe out doubts for yourself. Watch the raindrops sink into the ground, nurturing the area around you.

4. Close your eyes and listen to the rain pattering. Focus on its voice. Walk around the bowl. What is the rain saying? Does something inside you whisper anything about it?

5. Turn and retrace your steps, walking around the bowl in the opposite direction. Feel the rain falling on your body. Focus on that sense of touch.

6. Now kneel before the bowl and dip your fingertips in water that has collected. Visualize the water as a well of nutrients that nourish your inner guide, those instincts that lead you to be who you need to when unsure of yourself.

7. Take up the bowl. Hold it up to the sky. Whisper, chant, or sing of allowing the rains to call out your deeper instincts.

8. Drink the water, drop the bowl, and stand with arms up to the sky. Listen to your higher self. When energies are spent go home and drink a warm beverage for grounding purposes.

SNOW SPELL TO SHARPEN INSTINCTS

MATERIALS NEEDED: Snowy day, small outdoor space, a stick, yourself

TO PREPARE: Watch the snow fall. Bundle up before going outdoors.

THE WORK:

1. Go to an outdoor space after accumulation has covered the ground. Bring or find a stick.

2. With the stick in your dominant hand, reach up to the sky. Watch the snowflakes drift down on you. Breathe in the stillness. Marvel at the change in atmosphere.

3. Reach down. Tap the stick in front of your feet. See the change in the land.

4. Now draw a circle around yourself. Sit on the ground in the circle. Close your eyes and focus the mind on seeing your surroundings without the use of eyesight. Visualize the landscape, the falling snow. Listen for movement, sniff the air. Feel the wind, if there is any.

5. Hold the stick to the sky. Whisper, chant, or sing about finding inner truths that lead to better outward understandings.

6. Open your eyes and use the stick to draw your name in the snow. As something given by family, names are not the entirety of who we are but they are still rooted in everyone's being. Now draw a picture or

symbol that represents you above it. Beneath it write your favorite letter or number.

7. Meditate on these images. Let them connect inside of you and sharpen the traits and aspects of the higher self. Then rub your hands through the images. Symbols are just physical representations; like us, they are not meant to live forever but the meaning endures.

8. Lie back in the snow to ground yourself back in reality.

HAIL SPELLS FOR INSTINCTUAL STRENGTH

MATERIALS NEEDED: Hailstorm, a small outdoor space, small bowl, self

TO PREPARE: Hailstorms are often random and unpredictable, so this spell is simple and quick. Like moments where we must rely on our instincts, there is little time to prepare.

THE WORK:

1. Right after a hailstorm, go outside. Make sure the weather is safe (hail sometimes accompanies tornadoes) to avoid potential danger.

2. Fill a small bowl with as many hail balls as possible. Kneel before the bowl and pick up one of the balls. Raise it to the sky. Envision its power. Feel the energy surrounding it. Place it on the ground beside the bowl. Raise up each piece of hail focusing on them one by one while holding them high. Line them up beside the bowl.

3. Close your eyes. Roll the balls on the ground with your hands. Let the friction of the movements create an energy that connects your senses to the icy precipitation. As the energies build, move your hands faster until your body feels fully charged.

4. Stop and meditate on the sounds, smells, and sensations around you. Take up one of the hail balls with your eyes closed. Lightly lick it and place it in the bowl. Visualize the energies rushing down your tongue and into your body to strengthen your deeper instincts. Repeat with each. (Depending on the size, some may melt.)

5. Let the balls melt completely and then pour the water over your hands, half over one then half over the other.

6. Lie back in the snow to ground yourself back in reality.

5
SLEEPING OUTDOORS

Our instincts drive us to remember our place in nature. To find the balance between domesticity and the wild world, we must get back to the elements without modern comforts and seek out the answers hidden in the ancient knowledge gazing at us from the greenery.

It is one thing to tend a garden or go hiking and swimming; both activities lend people the means to be healthier and tap into stronger energies, but sleeping outside the home offers more.

Camping trips and stargazing excursions strengthen the ability to instinctually sense danger or friendliness in an area. Even just the backyard camp-outs that I've had with my children when they were toddlers exposed us all to the possibilities that life outside can offer. The wonder and adventure hiding in the grasses opened our senses. I myself prefer rougher terrain. Exploring remote campgrounds with activities requiring higher skill levels brings me closer to my instinctual self and reminds me to appreciate the comforts of home upon returning.

Getting outside for long periods of time and sleeping outdoors is an exercise that builds trust in ourselves. When confident in our instincts, we can better judge interactions and potential outcomes of interactions between family members, communities, nations, and beyond.

Exposure is a real concern. When outdoors, a person must be well prepared. Bringing the right company and supplies means the difference between a successful endeavor or failure. Research from varying sources also offers guidance to create favorable odds.

Once prepared, going outdoors to test yourself and your subconscious is rewarding. Wisdom grows. Discovering the ability to survive of one's own accord guides inquiring minds to brilliance.

Exposure

Getting acquainted with sleeping out of doors and building the prowess to survive by one's own skills takes practice. Instead of knowing how to build a house or what to gather from the moment we are born, the disadvantage of being human remains our lack of development.

Keeping track of my direction leads to a better awareness of my surroundings. Learning to read the stars and anticipate weather patterns is a matter of experience. The world comes alive when properly navigated. I forget life's pressure and find beauty in simplicity, meaning in necessity, and power in protection. Taking it further and infusing my own energies in a new area often touches me to my very core. I carry those energies within afterward and use them in my later workings.

The after-effects of overnight outdoor excursions remain with us. The bonds that deepen with nature and the universe are timeless. Like heroes from folklore, those who walk among the wild with respect and admiration find enlightenment and balance on their quests.

Begin with simple outdoor meditations, then hikes, swims, and other trips to form a solid base of information that allows growth. Anyone can set up a temporary campsite or resting area just on their own porch or backyard. Limited resources or abilities will not keep you from this great experience.

Once mastered, trusting the inner voice and the spirit of the surrounding areas brings spiritualists to new revelations. As always, it is necessary to remember personal limits and issues. Practicing these exercises in small groups with trusted friends is best for beginners and intermediates. As progress and experience continue, the occasional solitary journey leads to more findings and heightened abilities.

Preparing the Body

There are various outward and inward preparations that should be done in order to create a successful excursion sleeping in the open. The body must be in some kind of proper shape, or at least readied if one is hindered. An overnight trip spanning multiple days should be treated as a quest.

All endeavors are part of the greater journey. A person's awareness of their progress or regression is based on their level of self-awareness and of their surroundings.

When we are well versed in outdoor adventures, the prospect of danger and nature-related concerns is lessened. But there is more to it than that. The proper supplies, physicality, and state of health must be obtained before the body is ready to face the wild world openly.

To prepare the body:

1. Obtain physical paper maps in case of dead zones. Get a general idea of the lay of the land.

2. Study the weather of the area and pack appropriate clothing. Boots, raincoats, hats, gloves, etc. are often more important than they seem.

3. Bring enough food and water, but never too much as that will add weight for the trip into the site. There is a special skill to taking only what is needed.

4. Test the body. Go outside frequently and be aware of strengths and weaknesses.

5. Make sure to have a good sleeping sack, and bring a tent or covering just in case of extremely harsh weather. Even a good tent will ease the tension of the strongest storm.

Preparing the Mind

To heighten the senses, meditation and hikes are necessary. My mind is stronger when I explore different future surroundings and possibilities. I study maps and find information on the area beforehand to give myself a good idea of what will be required of me. It builds anticipation while also offering protective powers.

The energies built when readying myself lead to deep meditation that requires longer spans of time and patience. This is an exercise that extends the self beyond one's current location to reach out for the future one.

To prepare the mind for isolation and ward off delusional paranoia:

1. Take the night before your departure to reflect on where you have been. Imagine other past trips in the open, no matter how short. Recall any animal excursions and what you learned from those moments.

2. Read nonfiction materials from explorers modern and classic. Let their knowledge fill in the blanks where yours is not yet developed.

3. Before bed, walk through your home. Memorize it, every angle, each flaw. Appreciate all it has meant even when taken for granted.

4. Go to sleep, comfortable in your own bed. Know that when you return, you will be the same person just with more wisdom. Remember that plenty of people have wandered the earth without proper food, clothing, or shelter and survived. Resilience lives in everyone—we just have to find it.

Preparing the Spirit

There is a calming effect that comes with spiritual quests. Just before embarking, the period of uncertainty is thrilling. Hope and fear mingle, offering balance. The spirit is fed by this great energy and hosts enough light to serve as guidance through the heights of anxiety. I love facing the unknown. As a child my adventurous spirit sometimes got me into trouble, but each cut and scrape taught me lessons. I have carried these experiences with me.

It's best not to expect a perfect trip. Mistakes can be made without serious injury or issues so long as anyone undertaking a journey understands the need to shift focus when problems present themselves. Keep your expectations soft but your instincts sharp. For example, when coming upon a snake in the road, a panicked reaction will more likely result in catastrophe. Find the strength within to accept that the wild world holds many secrets; it is essential to do what is necessary to remain cautious. Moving in this manner will make you more able to handle yourself in many situations, or veer away from danger when needed.

To prepare for spiritual answers:

1. When preparing to sleep the night before, lie down but first visualize the trip: think of what tests lie waiting in the wilderness. See yourself meeting whatever comes with the fierce vitality of your ancestors.

Know that you are capable of more than the simple paths civilization has laid out.

2. Meditate on the dangers you have faced in the human-made constructs surrounding you—they are far more damaging that what awaits. For even if a person loses themselves to beast or storm, at least they go back to the earth as they were made to go.

3. Ponder mortality. Know that despite the need and will to survive, any journey could be our last. Do not hide from this truth—focus on it. Look beyond it. What comes from the after energies? Get past the emptiness and the unknown; go further. There is an electricity in this journey that leads to a fearlessness that offers protection to those who do not turn away from the truth of life.

Engaging

Exploring new surroundings exercises the body and the being. This kind of excursion calls for isolation. Communications devices other than pen and paper need to be left behind. One cannot fully disconnect from modern pressures while checking messages or staring at a screen.

While thus disengaged with technology and attuned with nature, the brain receives new insights. The journey begins with the body and pushes the mind to a more expansive universe. No two quests are alike, but many visits to the wild have peaks that must be met. In order to experience the full effects of your time at this site, all facets of your identity must be included. When first arriving:

1. Hike the surrounding areas. Enjoy the mystery. Keep a map and compass handy in case of lengthy turns or undesignated byways.

2. Pay attention to the wind and the sounds around the space. Listen and learn what each rustle of noise means.

3. Get to know the cloud formations, if any. Gaze long distances and teach your eyes to discern distance based on what is between you and the object you are focusing on. Look for tracks on the ground, scratches on tree trunks, or chewed down plants.

4. Sniff the air. Suck in each breath and taste the scent of other creatures. Get to know the differing flavors. Over time, a person better trained in this can even smell or taste fear, urgency, and so on.

5. Set up camp. Keep food and water contained and away from animals. Make sure any spare clothing is protected. Keep a first aid kit within reach in case of emergency.

6. Build a fire at mealtime. Make sure it is contained. A circle of rocks on a flat space of dirt is always preferred.

Familiarizing

Getting to know a new space helps us become more bonded to the land. Setting up camp and memorizing certain aspects of the landscape quells anxiety while offering prospects for exploration.

As I become familiar with a new outdoor space, I often find the need to build a fire and eat, drink, and laugh before it to truly connect with my surroundings. No matter where I am, those aspects of life must come with me. This early stage of camping hosts important powers that lend me heightened abilities. Using that power to meditate strengthens ties to the area and the world beyond.

As the sun grows heavy and night supersedes:

1. Walk around the site. Get to know the land's darker side. Utilize what you learned of the area to build trust with the dimly lit area around your fire.

2. Now go before the fire. Eat, drink, laugh, sing, dance, but all the while remain aware of the space.

3. Keep conscious of the wind, the scent of the night, the space beyond flame's light. How does it respond? Is the atmosphere tense, or friendly? Base your actions and celebration on the feel of the surrounding spans. Cease loud noises if danger calls, and keep close to the fire. Regardless of what happens keep the flames alive.

Connecting

When night falls, the atmosphere changes. No matter what space a person is exploring, the nocturnal world is a realm all its own. As the sky darkens, building a big fire proclaims territory to wildlife so they keep a safe distance. It also offers guidance.

The thrill of the day pounds in my veins whenever I sit before a large campfire. I like to exert myself hiking, swimming, and fishing before settling down to a more meditative state. For others who are less active or unable, simply sitting in the open air telling stories or taking a short walk harbors the same power to enlighten.

What truly matters is that a relationship has been established between a visitor and the land. Then a stronger meditation can begin. In the stillness of the late air:

1. Sit before the fire. Watch the flames slither about each other. Witness the wood or plants being eaten up like a meal. Ponder it. How are humans any different? All creatures work to survive. It is how we thrive.

2. Think of your work. Your job. Your endeavors. Regardless of what they fulfill, they too in essence keep you alive. Correlate the entire habitat you are visiting to your usual daily life. How does it differ? How is it similar?

3. Now look to the flames and meditate on your purpose in it all. Think of this quest in itself.

4. Lie back on the ground and gaze at the stars or empty sky. If there are stars, can you read them? What do they mean? Where do they lead? Let the mind wander but with direction. If there are no stars, stare into the dark depths. How does the blackness shape the span above? Does it say anything to you? Where does it come from? How does it shadow your life?

After-effects

The morning after sleeping on the ground starts off a little stiff. Stretching exercises will awaken the body and should present a stronger aspect. Some may stir from the fire. The coals will be warm enough to reignite, if not still going in some places. The clean air offers a perfect beginning.

It is customary to rebuild the fire for breakfast, but not required. The main thing to do is continue focusing on your surroundings. Keep the senses alert.

A splash of water on the face can do wonders. However one wakes up, once the grogginess is gone, a morning hike will better bond the spirit to this quest. Retracing the steps taken before a night in the open leads toward full recognition:

1. Pay attention to the wind and the sounds around the space. Listen and decipher what each noise means.

2. Reassess cloud formations (if any). Gaze long distances and remind your eyes to discern distance based on what is between you and the object you are focusing on. Look for fresh tracks on the ground, scratches on tree trunks, or chew marks on plants. Imagine what has visited the land since your hike the day before.

3. Sniff the air. Suck in each breath and taste the scent of other creatures; really work on learning the differing flavors.

Revisiting

Going back over yesterday's footsteps binds the body to the newly designed mind. It connects alternate pathways for the spirit and the future. Pack up all your belongings and clean the area to be better than it was before you came to it. If trash was left behind from someone else, pick it up and dispose of it. Part of the quest is accepting that life is unfair and there will be times when the carelessness and ignorance of others must be met with your power.

When it is time to leave, take one last look at your site:

1. Think of how it differs from when you arrived.

2. As you leave reflect on everything you experienced. What sights remain printed on the mind? What sensations still tickle the skin or cause your nose to grimace? How did your instincts aid you?

3. Now visualize how these experiences are utilized in society. How can you better listen to your instincts in more populated areas?

Returning

Once home, get everything put away first. The chore of unpacking is a huge drain on the body, but it only becomes worse the longer it is put off. I sometimes have to force myself to do it, but afterward I lie on my couch or bed and re-center myself and my focus based on my experiences, whether for a long nap or just a few minutes. Try the following practice to aid in this re-centering:

1. Breathe deep. Do you notice anything different? Stare at the ceiling, hear every noise, feel the energy of the room. It may feel more alive. It may not. But some change should be noticed.

2. Now Close your eyes. Focus on how the body feels in relation to this well-known area as opposed to the open space. Relax the mind and let the spirit wander back to where it slept the night before.

3. Focus on the different energies. Visualize them coming together as if your bed is in the wild or the wild is your backyard. They are related if not close together. Meditate on this and finish the quest.

Survival

Exposing yourself to unknown threats in the wilderness is different each time. Some trips will be successful, some will have issues. Then there are the times when a person may be faced with a matter of survival. What occurs is often based on multiple factors: preparation, location, weather supplies, and timing.

An individual or small group can control certain elements. Starvation and dehydration will not take place for those who bring enough provisions. Falls or injuries from steep hikes, drop-offs, rough terrain, and blocked paths are less likely to occur if those involved take care to explore the land with caution and respect. Picking the proper time of year to avoid voluminous migration patterns, interference with mating seasons, or even bad weather also aids in avoiding unnecessary peril.

Unexpected danger may surprise an explorer, but it is the reaction that determines whether they outlive it. The body may be sound, but if the mind is not it can spell disaster. How one approaches their abilities is important.

Branching away from the familiar to seek out different perspectives, methods, and information better grooms an explorer for unpredictable settings. Books cannot teach a person everything; they are like recipes. The reader must first get a feel for the idea and try mixing things together themselves to gain the outcome they wish for. Our hands are tools. Our brains are blueprints. The balance is keeping up with innovation while also remembering and practicing what came before in order to cultivate self-trust.

Instinct

When one does not know what to believe or what to trust, their instincts are all they have to rely on. Everyone has the power to sway their fate, and collectively the fate of humanity within those turns. The only place to find truth is in nature, but just visiting it for a hike or a swim is not full submersion.

Knowledge is about opening the self to outside information, but instincts rely on only what lies inside. When combined, it is easier to spot patterns to distinguish sincerity from disguised mockery. A person needs to be alone with their thoughts and the world that inspires them from time to time. Exposure to the dangers of the wild pulls forth inner sources of strength, thus allowing application in any scenario, but it is best for them to remain active even after returning to society.

To survive the wild, a person only needs their instincts. They are the cure for emptiness and what protects the subconscious and leads the spirit to wisdom. However, incorporating instincts after returning home takes a conscious effort. To aid in applying instinct in society, the following exercise may help:

1. Wake but do not rise right away. Give yourself time to be ready for the world. This means any alarms should be set to allow for this extra time.

2. Get up and go about your morning routine. Once on the way to wherever it is you generally go (even if staying home), think about all that must be done throughout the day. Sort through what is most important and why.

3. Visualize working through these tasks and the rewards that come after. If there is no reward, make or find one. All tasks, even the most menial, hold some kind of return.

4. Begin the day with purpose. When unexpected events or problems occur, trust your body. If your stomach twists, think of what eases it. If your head throbs, listen. It is trying to tell you something. When the heart changes its tempo, be aware of your surroundings, build your energies, and let instinct guide you.

Subconscious

Tapping into the hidden information which rests inside takes skill but allows the instincts to flourish and grow. A person is more whole when they remain aware of the subconscious and trust in its ability. Going into the wild to test this is a survival skill that is less intense than the lessons that come with sharper instincts.

When camping, my needs take precedence over wants (as they should). When forcing my mind to forget the comforts of technology and human-made trinkets, my subconscious slips closer to the forefront and ideas that were hidden surface to illuminate elements that best suit me.

To speak with the subconscious:

1. Exert the body. Hike, or dance around the campfire.

2. Either withhold food and drink before the activity (for long enough to get famished, but not enough to cause the body harm) or imbibe in some wine, absinthe, or other simple natural enhancers like mushrooms or ayahuasca (if legal in the area traveled to).

3. Clear the mind and let it guide you where it wants to. Give up control. Explore new thoughts and see where they lead.

Wisdom

Not every situation can be answered for, but resolutions are waiting to be found even when left open-ended. Wisdom is discovering peace and happiness in any situation or setting. Seclusion and the nondisruptive atmosphere of the wilderness provides a space for concentration. Deep thought is possible anywhere, but sheer unadulterated conceptualizing is best practiced in a space less traveled. When properly achieved, a sense of accomplishment and love flowers to fill a person with pure joy.

To follow wiser paths and lead with the spirit:

1. Take a moment during each phase of the day on your excursion to focus on small wonders. Morning, noon, afternoon, and night each host their own little enjoyments. Stop and put an emphasis on recognizing them. From flowers to birds, special treats or unexpected visitors, a person's perception of the world influences how they proceed through life. How

one looks at their campsite will determine how far their growth reaches on each journey.

2. While hiking, swimming, or exploring the area, think of what ails you. What is the worst part of this trip so far? Allow some time to acknowledge the annoyances or pains that arise from a quest of this magnitude.

3. Now think of what makes the excursion worthwhile. What is the best thing that has happened so far? Focus on that and let it be like a lucky charm in the form of a thought. Carry it with you for the rest of the adventure. It will attract more positive events.

4. Visualize balancing everything. Do not hide from negative energies, but remember the positive ones. Go throughout the rest of the hike or swim with the conscious effort to look beyond selfish endeavors. Instead of just focusing on refining the self, reach beyond and recall an instance where someone lashed out at you or others for no reason. Seek the main cause. Deduce what led them to that behavior. Most often, unexpected outbursts are the result of hidden wounds caused by previous damage. Did you offer neutrality or did you grow defensive? Whatever the response, think of what could be done to ease future situations. How can your behavior aid that of others?

Enjoyment

Getting out under the sky and letting the stars watch you sleep softens harsh realities while toughening those who could use a bit of shaping. Just because someone is on a quest for answers does not mean they must cast off pleasure. What dampens the mind and destroys a person's greater sense of purpose is growing obsessed with pleasure. When balanced, what we enjoy becomes what smooths out the wrinkles and reminds us to live wholeheartedly.

But enjoyment isn't just about clinging to our likes. It is about exploration and learning to appreciate even the aspects of life that are more difficult. Seeing more of the world and its happenings are special rites and rituals that can aid a person on a journey.

For those who are unable to leave home due to resources, injuries, disabilities, or timing, there is always a way to appreciate everything. When travel is not possible, sleeping outside the home is a perfect alternative.

Whether in a yard or on a porch or deck, just the act of freeing the body of a roof can have similar—if not the same—effects as sleeping in the wilderness. The range is limited, but there are other dangers and concerns that arise. From nocturnal scavengers drawn to human waste to intruders and ill-meaning humans, these threats are just as real as the ones hiding in natural areas.

When a person is more self-assured, they emit energies great enough to influence their future and even the universe. Much of what has been and will be is already displayed above. Reading the stars is not an easy task. It is a science that requires precision, training, and talent.

For Those Unable to Travel

Limitations are not a dead end. When facing difficulty with resources or health (among other things), there is always a way to continue on. Humans are resilient. When forced into constrictive situations, they will work harder to get beyond what delays their progress.

When deterred from traveling, sleeping out under an open sky is still a possibility. Whether in a yard or on a porch, deck, or stoop, it is possible for anyone who wishes to get closer to the heavens to do so. And in some rare circumstances, even simply opening a window all the way and removing any screens allows some of the effects that sleeping outside produces. The main things to remember are being conscious of physical or mental limitations, preparing to avoid further damage, and having faith in fate.

Relax and ease into this rite:

1. Do not pretend to be more agile than you are. Get to your sleeping space and lay out your sleeping bag (or if in a wheelchair or other assisting device, grab whatever blankets are needed).

2. Look to or touch the part of the body that hinders travel. Focus on it. Visualize everything it has stopped you from doing and all the disappointment it has caused in the past or present.

3. Now gaze up to the sky. If it looks clear, focus on that darkness and imagine all the negative energies being sucked away. If the night is starry, focus on one star. Examine its luster. Is it brighter or darker than the others? Is it alone? Let the star represent yourself. How does

it shine? Where does its power come from? Would it cease to be if a single piece was broken or destroyed, or would it continue on?

4. Now think of what a star is. It is gas, flatulence. People lend those burning rocks mysticism and hope while they fart through life. Let yourself laugh at that notion. Find the hilarity of your own situation (and of any companions, if present). Remember that although a fool may seem stupid, it is the person who has lost their sense of humor who is dead inside.

5. Sing, dance, clap, hum, spin, raise your arms and shake them at the sky: do whatever inspires lighthearted silliness. Imbibe in wine, absinthe, or other raw natural enhancers (check about drinking etc., if on medication).

6. Let your spirit be proud of the body it inhabits. It is yours and no one else's. Treasure that intimate relationship and meditate on it. Talk to the sky. Do not be afraid of vulnerability.

7. Sleep. If restless, take periods of waking to meditate and speak with the god(s) or your energies. Do not ignore signs of complications. If you need to go back indoors, do so. This rite can be attempted at another time or performed inside on a smaller scale.

Finding One's Place

No matter what level of physicality a person achieves, they have a purpose and a place on this earth. Figuring out specific meaning comes easier for some than others. Everyone is different.

A sense of not belonging develops in everyone at some point. It is part of our journey through nature and society. No matter how similar humans can be, everyone has their own unique fingerprints.

Instead of fixating on when I was hurt, left behind, or unable to fit in, it was a love of myself and my oddities that gave me happiness. I do not sit still well. I'm dyslexic and strong-willed. When I focus on something like music, art, or gardening, I find true freedom with or without the approval of others, but I wasn't born that way. I had to move beyond self-doubt and ridicule.

Concepts are easy when laid out, but applying and practicing them is the test of will. It is much easier to understand and love the self when stepping away from outside expectations. Sleeping outside like the elements that make us develops a stronger sense of self. It exposes the gods, or the powers that be, in new ways.

To leave behind past grievances and enjoy who you are during this journey:

1. Take off your socks and shoes, boots, or sandals; all footwear must be removed.

2. If you are wearing long sleeves, roll them up.

3. Take off any headgear, eyewear, etc.

4. If it is warm enough, remove all attire as you are comfortable. Complete nudity is a plus if permitted (and not embarrassing).

5. Turn to the north and spread legs. Raise arms up and out to the sides. Breathe in and feel the air bathing the skin. Now shake your body. Be ridiculous. Get silly. Do not be afraid to look or act like a fool. Laugh at yourself and your surroundings.

6. Turn to the south and do the same thing, but this time, dance about if feeling up to it. Magic is not all bowing and stiffness. Those concepts belong in man-made oppressive constructs. The spirit requires more creativity and playfulness. One cannot be happy with themselves or learn their purpose if they lock their limbs in simple positions.

7. Close your eyes and spin until you are dizzy. Fall on the ground if you must.

8. Run hands over arms, legs, head, neck, shoulders, chest, and torso. (Masturbatory or sexual energies can be used here, but keep focused on the end goal.) Feel the familiarity. Ground yourself in the body you were born to. Laugh at its flaws and smile at its grandeur.

9. Lie back and watch the world roll before your eyes. Absorb its constant motion. Clouds pass or birds fly, the sun moves across the sky. Life is motion. Without some kind of mobility, humans grow stagnant. Meditate on that. Focus the mind on what positive endeavors make you feel most alive and how you can incorporate that joy into less agreeable subjects.

10. When your thoughts have grown exhausted, sit up and get a snack and some water. You may not be 100 percent certain of everything, but you

should grow closer as the subconscious absorbs what has taken place and the spirit revives the energies expelled in this odd practice.

11. Repeat as needed.

Stargazing

Stargazing holds magical properties that are not just based in astrology. For the less versed in skyward maps, lights twinkling overhead host other energies. Star meditations take a person from their mortal body and project the spirit above and beyond. The paths that appear as a result of exploring spiritual elements that connect humanity to the cosmos lead in every direction. There are revelations for every skill set and spells for those who seek out heightened influence.

Wishing on a star is a light spell. Akin to prayer, it all comes from the same place: that part of ourselves that is more entwined with the entirety of existence.

Deeper, refined spellwork is available to spiritualists who seek it. Within those rites remains the power to gaze beyond time, find good fortune, and even experience the universe and its creator(s) with more definition. Not everyone can master communicating with the stars, but all of us have the ability to tap into heightened energies to better thrive.

No matter how one looks upon the stars, they possess a direct link to all beings and the planets the shimmer above around. Everything is written in the stars. Figuring out how to decipher them is a skill with a long past. It is an art.

One does not have to become a scholar or dedicated scribe to the universe in order to build a stronger relationship with the universe. When adventuring outside, sleeping beneath the stars is a perfect opportunity to expand one's knowledge of constellations, planetary positioning, and the bonds that attract our energies to space. To prepare, research is encouraged, as is contacting well-versed astrologers if possible.

After going to the site and exploring other avenues of adventure, a calming meditation is customary to release tension and create a relaxing experience.

1. Gaze up into the sky. Visualize the magnitude of each star and planet above.

2. Try to identify any or all constellations present. Meditate on how those images have guided others before you. Imagine yourself as one of those

past beings and how life has changed. Then think of the aspects of existence that continue on no matter what events or discoveries occur.

3. Now find your star; everyone has one. It is the star that best represents you and your vision for your future self. If you have the knowledge, follow your path based on the stars above and listen to them. What do they say?

Fate

Fate is never sealed until consecrated by the actions carried out in life. Expanding the mind beyond the body comes after the calming meditation. The stars are no stranger to laugher—like the god(s)/fates, they enjoy the ride.

Listening to the stars may provide insights, but they should not weigh too heavily on the mind. Trusting in what is meant to be is an act of faith that has gone out of style. Getting back to nature and the lands without technologies that hold numerous answers at the click of a button is an act of faith in itself. Practicing that act expands a person's thoughts. Instead of boxing the self into modern ideals, new possibilities open and clear options present themselves.

To take advantage of this mindset:

1. Light a fire or sit before one already blazing. Gaze up into the sky, but remain conscious of the warmth provided.

2. Trace the patterns and shapes above with your prominent pointer finger.

3. Think of their glow as an energy drawing nearer every second. Visualize that power touching your finger, going into it. Let it fuse internally.

4. Close your eyes and see the stars. Follow them. Let them lead you through your thoughts and into new ideas and interests.

The Cosmos

No matter what is written in the stars, everyone holds the power to meet their fate in their own way if they will it strongly enough. Individual energies host one's unique qualities but also extend far beyond the self. A person can tap into higher powers because the two are linked.

There are differing methods to aid a person in looking beyond the self to reach out for others, our creator(s), and the universe itself. The stars are already charged. They provide a perfect focus to center the mind and expand the spirit. A complex meditation to stretch the spirit can be executed as follows:

1. Light a fire or stand before one already blazing in the open air. Gaze up to the sky and study the stars. Clear the mind.

2. Go through each star and focus on every single bright light one at a time. Let the warmth of fire forge a deeper connection to the burning rocks overhead. Let that heat move through your body. Feel it build your energies and coax the instincts from hiding.

3. With one hand reach for the fire. Get as close as possible without being burned. Now extend other hand to the sky. Align your fingers with the five brightest, most close-set stars.

4. Close your eyes and use the fire's warmth to visualize the heat burning off each twinkling star. Let the spirit drift from the body toward that cluster of stars. Single out one. Stretch your energies toward it. Float from the ground. See yourself leaving Earth in search of the rock that flashes its grin upon the world. Get as close to it as possible in spirit.

5. You may sweat, the heart may race, pound, or even swim. Imagine yourself as a star. Become one with it and the universe. Look upon the world and everything surrounding it. Gaze beyond what you "know" and look into what truly is.

6. When the star begins to cool that is a signal that your body is exhausted. Lie down on the ground and open your eyes. Ground yourself back in your body. Sit before the fire and breathe.

Spells

The freedom of the open air offers a perfect setting for spellwork. When sleeping outdoors, the stars hold more purpose. A fire burns brighter. Everything that we are comes together to connect body and mind with the spiritual.

STEPPING OUT OF TIME

MATERIALS NEEDED: Fire, a watch or sundial or other timepiece, starry night, self

TO PREPARE: Light a fire and practice the star meditations so you are fully prepared.

THE WORK:

1. Set the timepiece before the fire. Close your eyes and clear your mind. Think of time as a concept and what it means to you.

2. Walk around the fire counterclockwise starting at the timepiece, then clockwise returning to it.

3. Raise the timepiece up to the sky (or kneel before it if it is a garden statue sundial that is too heavy). Look to the stars. Focus on them in relation to the timepiece.

4. Close your eyes and visualize time as an energy. Let its vast expanse surround you. Open eyes and stare at a single star. Visualize it moving across your field of vision, backward for the past, forward for the future.

5. Set the timepiece before the fire. Raise arms to the sky and meditate on the stars. They should speak of times forgotten or reveal what is to be.

FINDING GOOD FORTUNE IN THE STARS

MATERIALS NEEDED: Starry night, yourself (optinal: pen and paper or a camera)

TO PREPARE: Have a basic knowledge of constellations and planetary positions.

THE WORK:

1. Stand in a calm space outside and look to the sky.

2. Find familiar constellations and envision how they have been there for you even if you didn't know it. Imagine how many times Orion's Belt has glowed above nights filled with glee or the North Star has shimmered like a beacon.

3. Look for planets visible to the naked eye. Look to their glow and focus on how they are linked to every positive and negative energy in existence just as our planet and everything upon it is as well.

4. Sit down and focus on your energies. Make them increase and build. Feel them warm your insides, coat the brain.

5. Lie back and visualize yourself as a glowing entity. Like a star or planet you have your own gravitational pull. You have your own path and

purpose. Set your mind to that purpose. Meditate on clearing your way
to achieve what you know must be done.

6. Now open your eyes. Raise pointer finger of both hands and trace new
constellations in the stars overhead. Let them represent the phases and
/or stages of your will in accordance with that of the god(s) and the
universe.

7. Afterward close your eyes and fold your hands over your chest. Imagine
your purpose being fulfilled before your body is done in this life. If you
feel compelled, sit up and record the new constellations with pen and
paper, or take a picture of the sky.

DRAWING POWER FROM THE STARS

Materials Needed: Fire, large stick or staff, starry night, self

To Prepare: Light a fire and stoke it with the stick or staff that will be used for
this rite.

The Work:
1. Stand before the fire with the stick or staff. Clear your mind and focus
on pouring your energies into it.

2. Hold the staff up to the sky. Whisper, sing (and dance), or chant to
the stars. Ask them to see you, draw their undivided attention in your
direction.

3. Close your eyes and feel their power. Visualize your energies extending
through the tip of your staff to meet the power of the cosmos. Expand
your energies and weave them around that of the stars. Pull it down,
down, down, and back to the earth like a fishing pole bringing in a
catch.

4. Lower the staff and stand it before you, between yourself and the fire.
Let the bottom end rest on the ground. Balance on it slightly. Now
press the free, upright tip to your forehead as you keep it standing.
Bend or adjust as needed.

5. Absorb the newly charged energies through the head. Feel them trick-
ling through the rest of the body, surging through the blood in your
veins. Let the charge electrify your body.

6. Now focus that energy on fulfilling your purpose, mending your fears with your hopes. The body may tingle. The head will grow heavy or light; it will definitely feel different.

7. Drop to your knees and hold the staff horizontally between your hands. Bow to the fire. Meditate on it and your new sensations. Ground yourself back to the earth by recognizing your physical state, but keep your heightened sense of being.

BOOSTING KARMA WITHIN THE COSMOS

MATERIALS NEEDED: Self and the stars

TO PREPARE: Practice the star meditations and have a basic knowledge of constellations and planetary positions.

THE WORK:

1. Walk beneath the stars. Think of your main issues requiring resolution, lacking closure or justice. Focus on balance and what is truly fair.

2. Now look to the stars. Recognize familiarities. Greet known constellations and visible planets like old friends. Call on their energies to guide and aid you.

3. Spread legs as wide as possible. Raise arms up to the sky but reaching apart like a human star shape. Close your eyes and pull your power from within. Let it build and expand through your body like a bomb ready to explode.

4. Visualize the end to the issue, the full karmic balance that rights everything again. See it taking place. Illuminate that image with your glowing energies.

5. Stare into the stars and whisper, sing, or scream a chant/call to force a balance through. Everything rights itself in time, but this will nudge the resolution quicker for your safety and/or well-being. (Like most spells, this one is meant only to be used when absolutely necessary, when no amount of action or reasoning has created any peace.)

HEALING OLD WOUNDS WITH STARWORK

MATERIALS NEEDED: Small bowl of water, fire, handful of dirt or sand, a large stick or staff, and the self

TO PREPARE: Bless the items to be used by meditating on them and pushing your energies into the objects. Build and start a fire. Stoke the flames with the staff.

THE WORK:

1. Place items before you facing the fire. Kneel. Clear your mind and gaze up at the sky. If it is starry, focus on the brilliance of each light one by one. If completely dark, concentrate on the encompassing vastness above and how it too holds a great beauty when just looming with inky quietude.

2. Grab the bowl of water and stare down into the clear element. See yourself staring back, no matter how faint, it is a true representation. Set the bowl between knees and dip your fingertips in. Close your eyes and visualize your pain. Dwell on the old wounds (mental or spiritual) that somehow remain open. Bring them to the surface.

3. Open your eyes and visualize what happened on top of the water.

4. Take a handful of dirt. Clench it in your fist and feel its neutralizing powers, its ability to seal negative energies for good. Drop it into the water.

5. Slowly stand and take up the staff. Grip it tight and hold it over the bowl horizontally. Close your eyes and build your energies. Pour them into the staff.

6. Then stare above. Stretch the tip of your stick overhead vertically.

7. Let your power extend through the far end and call upon the sky or the stars through a whisper, chant, song, or yell. Make the universe hear your call. Draw its power down from the cosmos into the end of your staff.

8. Now flip the pole and touch the charged end of the stick into the dirty water. Swirl it clockwise and counterclockwise. Visualize the energy

within the staff going into the contents, mixing until the dirt has covered the water with its power.

9. Lay the staff before the bowl and lift the vessel. Hold it up to the sky. Dump the mixture over the flames, slowly.

10. Sit before the fire and meditate on completing your healing process.

A STAR BINDING

MATERIALS NEEDED: Fire, pen and paper, self

TO PREPARE: Build the fire. (May be cast directly before the spell for Boosting Karma within the Cosmos or on its own.) Write the name of the person(s) you are binding. If working on your own, fill the page with their name; for small groups, repeat in a pattern until the page is full. (If done in a large group, writing each name once is appropriate. But something of this magnitude is not advised unless absolutely necessary.)

THE WORK:

1. Go before the fire with the list. Gaze to the sky and meditate on the stars or the darkness if none are shining. Focus the mind on communicating your energies through those of the world, and the cosmos. Listen and let the universe speak to you.

2. Turn your attention to the fire and visualize it as a part of the stars. Focus on its power as the flames continue to move about.

3. Whisper, sing, chant, or shout words to bind the responsible party from doing more harm. Read and repeat the name(s). Let the warmth inside you grow and grow until your energies feel ready to burst.

4. Whisper, sing, chant, or shout to seal the binding using the same pattern spoken before but utilizing the name(s) this time.

5. Fold the paper in half. Fold that half in half. Continue folding the paper in half until it can be condensed no more. Bring it to your lips. Kiss it while visualizing the subject(s) unable to cause any more pain.

6. Hold the folded paper up to the sky. Push the name(s) and the image of its/their owner(s) out through your mind.

7. Return focus to the fire and toss the list in. Visualize the harming element burning away from the person(s) on the list. See them coming to terms with what they've done and carrying the burden of their scars and those they imparted on others, whether physical, mental, or spiritual.

8. Sit back and meditate on your role in all of it.

6
FIRE

Fire has a deep connection to humanity. It can harm or heal. It inspires and terrifies. It is a perfectly balanced entity with cleansing properties. Cooking over an open flame is sacred. The simple act binds people to their heritage, but that is not all the power fire has in regards to medical benefits. There are meditations and practices that teach a body to heal itself. These are more potent when incorporating fire.

Spellwork often requires a fire even if not rooted in the flames. Earth, air, and water can be found or represented in many forms, but fire is more limited. Candles, fireplaces, or outdoor pits are available to everyone in at least one of those three forms, but they need tending and a careful eye.

Fire scrying has a rhythm like a beating pulse. Time is hidden within the flames and can bend like liquid metal. Scrying with this element is a difficult process that demands full concentration. Meditation aids in practice, as does spellwork. No matter how prepared you believe you are, the act and experiences that come from it are otherworldly. It is best to expect nothing and appreciate whatever is revealed.

Whether seeking peace with the past, guidance in the present, or the wisdom of the future, fire scrying wraps all aspects of my being into one solid mass. It helps me focus even when my brain feels like it is hosting a festival of ideas. The level of skill required for this particular practice is beyond meditation and simple spellwork. You must be well versed in reading instincts, and your subconscious must already have been tested to at least a small degree.

Clearing Spaces

Contained fires are perfect for cleaning a work space before spellwork, meditations, or a dirty kitchen or home. The smoky scent of fire mingled with wood holds much meaning for everyone. It reaches through barriers.

Lighting a fire doesn't just scent the air or push away negative energies; it prepares the body for stillness. I am better able to find a comfortable position when gazing at the flames and warming the skin. It guides my mind to let go of unnecessary chatter. Woes and worries slip to the wayside in favor of peace and reprieve. The instincts within are stirred more evenly, creating a consistent higher being which is able to reach out to further energies.

Fires produce the perfect atmosphere for meditation. Focus is better guided before glowing embers.

To direct the focus on cleansing the body/ridding the self of bad habits:

1. Light a candle or build a small fire.

2. Sit before the flame(s) in a comfortable position (away from any wind if doing an outdoor fire). Clear the mind.

3. Focus on the flame(s). Let the dancing heat burn itself into your mind. Think of how extreme temperatures kill germs, bacteria, and negative energies—they reset everything.

4. Now visualize yourself as the flame. Think of the heat coating your skin like a washcloth and moving over the surface to clear away all unwanted dirt. Feel it destroy the common cold, flues, and all viral illnesses. See it purify the pores and lend the body strength. (If you are not needing to break a bad habit, draw back and clear the mind once more, grounding the self in reality before finishing.)

5. Fixate on that strength until it becomes a power. Build these energies until they seep into the entire body. If wishing to rid certain habits, envision the action now. Look at it as clearly as possible, leaving nothing out. Now is not the time to hold back.

6. Raise the flames over this idea playing through your mind. Make them engulf the habit and burn away its necessity.

7. Beneath the ashes dig for the catalyst. Burn that out as well. Get rid of all the residue until the mind and body are ready to leave the habit behind.

8. When empowered to free yourself completely, pull back and blink at the flame(s). Watch the fire for a few minutes with a clear mind. Let the projected fire in your mind cool. Bow to the fire source.

Finding Focus

The mind is trickier; thoughts are fluid, sometimes rushing as strongly as a river until something plugs it up. When I feel out of focus, I have to work to steady the flow of thoughts and regain control:

1. Light a candle or build a small fire.

2. Sit before the flame(s). Get into a comfortable position (away from any wind if the fire is outdoors). Clear the mind.

3. Focus on the flame(s). Let the dancing heat warm your thoughts. See yourself as the fire.

4. Recall the woes and worries that have plagued you, one by one. With each uncertainty or negative memory, let the heat coat the idea in warmth. Look for the positive charge, the fuel that feeds the flames from this thought or occurrence.

5. Now engulf feelings of fear, anxiety, or depression in the flames. Make them rise in your mind. Destroy all that has cluttered your brain, but direct the fire around what must be kept. The goal is not to forget but to clean up the thought process to better analyze and control our thoughts.

6. As the weight is lifted from the mind, pull back from deep thought. Relax. Watch the light flicker. Clear the mind and meditate on the fire, slowly coming back to yourself in an act of grounding.

Forward Thinking

No one is ever truly cleared of the muck that accumulates through life. It is the messes we create, clean up, and sometimes walk into unknowingly that bring out our true nature. To polish what has been and look toward better endeavors:

1. Light a candle or build a small fire.

2. Sit before the flame(s). Get comfortable (away from any wind if doing an outdoor fire). Clear the mind.

3. Focus on the fire. Let the dancing heat grow within. Feel the fire within, let it grow. Build it up. Remain conscious of the energies as they warm.

4. Close your eyes. Envision the entire body engulfed in flame, sweating out the toxins that attack every aspect of being. Let the past surround you in tendrils of smoke. Greet it with balance. The pain and the joys brought you to this moment. Hug them in your mind, then let go of them.

5. Visualize yourself in the present—who you are, what you do with yourself and how you react to others. Are you happy with your role in life, or how you are treated?

6. Focus on pushing the flames toward all that you despise in yourself. Let the flames lick at your lesser traits and burn away the foundation they stand on. From the ashes replace the image with images of yourself acting out with the traits and habits you desire.

7. Look to the future and imagine where you are going. Is it healthy? Does it lead to fulfilling connections that last and can be carried through ages? Suffocate fears and self-destruction. Feed the ideas more fire. Fuel them with the heat residing within.

8. Pull back from deep thought and relax. Stare at the fire, let it bring you back to reality. Clear your mind and ground yourself in the here and now.

Healing Flames

The medicinal properties of fire are undisputed. From sweating out toxins, to neutralizing smoke and making use of flame as a focus for meditation, this element hosts varying methods toward bettering one's overall health.

When ailing from viruses, disease, or deeper issues, the power of fire is a trusted friend so long as it is used with caution and care. Before resorting to spellwork, deep meditation is always a wiser path. A person should never expel their energies in unnecessary ways. Home remedies like herbal concoctions are better for a first attempt. If those do not work, then deep fire meditations are most useful.

For best results, one should familiarize themselves with meditation in general and master the beginner and more intermediate practices before attempting to perform a healing meditation. Not only is it more effective, it's also safer. When pooling your energies exhaustion and misdirected powers can leave the less experienced individual worse off than when they began.

To heal a physical ailment:

1. Build a fire or light a candle and sit before the flame(s).
2. Close your eyes. Meditate on the issue plaguing your body. Fixate on the type of pain and how it affects you.
3. Now either grab the candle or take up a stick and hold it in the fire. Focus your energies on absorbing the healing flames through either the candle or the stick.
4. Slowly bring the candle or stick over the body and hold over area(s) that are doing poorly. Meditate on drawing the power of fire in through the area needing it most. Feel the heat block the pain and visualize the source healing.
5. Then sit back and smile on the flames.

To heal a mental ailment:

1. Build a fire or light a candle and sit before the flame(s).
2. Close your eyes. Meditate on the problems residing in thought and mental state. Recall how the mentality causes issues.
3. Now lean as close to the flame(s) as possible without scorching your skin. Let the head warm your face. Now draw it further in. Let it seep through the body into the brain and wrap around every idea and your consciousness like a warm blanket fending off frost.
4. Meditate on focusing the power of the fire on smoking out unwanted mental ailments or unhealthy thoughts. Feel negative thoughts dehydrate and evaporate. Visualize the mind growing stronger, healthier.
5. Now sit back and watch the flames.

To heal a spiritual ailment:

1. Build a fire or light a candle and sit before the flame(s).
2. Recall the issue or occurrence weighing you down.
3. Visualize the spiritual problem being thrown into the fire. Watch its meaning and catalyst reveal itself.
4. Focus your energies and extend them to the power displayed by the flames. Increase your power as your sense of being heals. Envision how you can better yourself in all ways to escape the negativity that was caused. See how your path is laid out and find a better way to walk it.
5. Sit back and watch the flames.

Cooking

And now for the fun part. Magic and fire are best friends. Together they inspire love, laughter, mystery, and a bit of sass. These are aspects of life I appreciate that help me refrain from falling into negative cycles or destructive behavior.

All great celebrations break away from the mundane. No two rituals are ever identical. The rites hold many meanings, but it is feasting which is the main course of holidays or gatherings. Universally accepted, cooking holds unique powers that touch everyone who tastes a handmade dish prepared with effort and care.

Depending on the method, different energies can be mixed and poured. Cooking outdoors is a stronger way to get in touch with nature and the planet. When using more domestic methods, stove-tops or oven cooking are modernized enough that anyone can find their way around a kitchen whether witch, Pagan, atheist, or a worshiper of monotheism.

When preparing and cooking food, I own my connection between survival and fueling the body. The warmth of a flame or the heat of an oven pleases the senses. The satisfaction of creating a meal with raw ingredients is experienced in full as my body absorbs the nutrients and transforms them into energy. That energy is charged to better lead my brain. This gives me control over my focus (or lack thereof).

The act of turning the ingredients or containing everything over flame puts me in a trancelike state. It is meditative. To draw forth cooking energies:

1. Light the grill or contained firepit.

2. Let the heat and smoke wash over you.

3. Meditate on the weather and its influence on the flames. Be thankful for the ability to cook.

4. When ready, place food over the flame whether using a grate, spit, or pot. Watch the flames lick at the food. See your hard work transform before your eyes and let it build your energies. Send the feelings of accomplishment, contentedness, or peace into the food for yourself and anyone who may partake of the meal with you.

5. Once the food is ready, remove, and extinguish the flames with gratitude. Present the food with pride and truly celebrate.

Modern Cooking

When baking or cooking dishes in the oven or on the stove-top, the same concept is still easily applied, but the energies that charge the food are more potent during preparation than the act of cooking.

1. Preheat the oven or start food prep for stove-top cooking.

2. Be aware of the increasing temperature in the room as you get everything ready.

3. Focus on the joys of dining with yourself after a hard day or that of being accompanied by friends and/or family. Think of the sense of peace and happiness that comes with being surrounded by love. Now expand that sensation. Feel its power like an electric charge and push it into the food as you make it.

4. When placing the dishes in or over heat for cooking, stare at the pan or oven and feel the warmth of this act; not just the physical warmth but also the mental comfort. Meditate on that.

5. Once the food is ready, remove and shut off the oven or burner with gratitude. Present the food with pride and truly celebrate.

Hearth Cooking

Hearth cooking is a lost art that has been rendered obsolete. The lack of necessity has led people to drift from the practice, but living in a log cabin or a self-sustaining home allows one to experience hearth cooking as a fun aspect of life.

Though not as common in today's world, cooking in a hearth serves as a link between age-old methods and what has become the norm in the past century. Anyone with a wood burning fireplace can still cook indoors the old-fashioned way. The energy in this action is just as great as when grilling or cooking outdoors because it is just as hazardous, if not more. If your home is equipped so that you can partake of this style of cooking, it is customary to remember to beware house fires and be prepared for emergencies. Use your fireplace to partake in this ancient work. Go at your own pace and slowly build your knowledge; do not rush anything. To start:

1. Build and light the fire. (If using a cauldron or pot for stew, put in place before lighting. The same goes for a spit, but if roasting something, the food needs to be put in place before the fire is started as well.)

2. Sit back and marvel at the heat and light the flames give off.

3. When ready, add the food to the pot, turn the food on the spit, or hold smaller covered pans or pots over the flames. Be careful to maintain a safe distance while also being close enough to stir or tend as needed.

4. While doing so, focus on the act of making this food, the time and energy it consumes. Now visualize that power as a sacrifice for yourself and the ones you care for. See your actions meet success and expand on that success by infusing the food with your positive energy.

5. Once the food is ready, remove and place on counter or table to cook for a moment. Go back before the flames and bow. Be thankful and marvel at your work.

6. Present the food with pride and truly celebrate.

Scrying

What separates scrying from the other practices is the necessity for escaping reality. Society grounds individuals for its purpose, a fact that is itself neither negative or positive—it all depends on how one responds to it. When presented with certain facts, it is important to remember that rules and scientific laws are often defined by people—"people" being the key word.

Listening to the warnings our instincts send out helps us know when to advertise all our secrets and when to whisper them quietly in the back of the mind. Scrying exercises this ability. It lends answers to questions unasked. It directs the seer better.

When attempting to scry, I find it imperative to build my own fire or at least have some hand in feeding the heat. Nothing will be revealed to anyone who is not practiced, open, or has a natural talent for it. So long as meditation and spellwork have returned positive results, scrying is a safe next step for anyone wishing to explore the unknown sciences and magic contained within the earth.

There are varying levels of fire scrying. The larger and more brilliant the blaze, the easier visions reveal themselves. My first successful scrying experience did not take me to the past or the future but showed me a helpful image of the present. I was away from my eldest child for the first overnight trip away and missed her terribly. The flames picked up on this feeling and showed me her activities at that moment. I later confirmed what I saw with my sister who was caring for her. I learned a lot from that experience. Instead of seeking specific images of a single moment in time or defined answers, I had to give up all preconceived notions and let the flames tell their story as they chose to do so.

Depending on the fire, a person can connect in different ways. My small to midsized campfire was most specific, but still wild. It did not wish to be defined.

When going before these kinds of flames, it is best to meditate first. Drawing the mind toward certain topics is more likely to reveal whatever is being sought than fully formed wishes and desires because our thought processes and the powers that exist around them are more complex than we may believe. The subconscious is better suited to converse with the elements to view scenes or hear secrets out of time. If you are wishing to learn of the past or the future, both are acceptable points of focus to vaguely draw out but once the trance takes over, what is shown is up to the universe.

Indoor fireplace scrying is highly intimate. The smaller and more contained the flame, the more work the practitioner must do. Fireplace and indoor fires work best like spellwork; instead of just meditating or focusing the mind, one must let go of their inhibitions while also keeping consciousness in check. The brain will warm and images may flash. What is important is that the person performing this rite enter the space with no doubts. It does no good to insult the flames. Faith and trust must be present. Chanting, positioning, and even some materials like sticks or crystals hold the power to enhance the connection and inspire a positive experience. What matters most is that whatever is shown or suppressed, you remember that you chose this attempt.

The last and most difficult aspect of fire scrying is single flame/candle magic. In spellwork and meditation, candles are a small step; they do not require much time and technique. For scrying, it is the opposite—the smaller the flame, the less potent the power to see beyond current realities. However, candles are no less important to scrying. Within them lies a test of strength and passion. When we are ready, single flame scrying may offer up highly defined, specific truths and answers.

Bonfire Scrying

Large bonfires are a perfect start to attempt scrying. They provide power, plenty of heat, and a mysticism that opens the senses to new possibilities. Best done after nightfall, the experience is mood altering. Once acquainted with the fire:

MATERIALS NEEDED: Wine, water, or natural enhancer (if desired); fire, self, stick

TO PREPARE: Build a bonfire or throw sticks into a fire already built to better connect with the element.

THE WORK:

1. Stand before the flames. Drink wine, water, or make use of other natural enhancers.

2. Take up a stick and hold it up to the fire. Study its shadowed aspect. Then throw it into the fire.

3. Dance around the blaze. Sing, laugh, and release all pent-up energies.

4. Find a welcoming spot to stop and gaze upon the bonfire.

5. Clear the mind but keep eyes open. Find your stick or focus on a different one. Watch as it burns. Feel the heat and trust its power.

6. Now focus on the flames. Stare at the center of the blaze. Really look at the middlemost part of the great fire.

7. Breathe deep. Listen to the hiss and sizzle of the fire. Each crack, each pop is a message. Decode that message by relaxing the eyes and ears. Instead of looking for contrast and definition let everything before you blur together.

8. Strange shapes may appear. Whispered words or strange sensations may occur. Let them come in their own time. Have patience. Let a trancelike state slowly consume you.

9. Do the flames produce images? What does the fire say? Find the freedom in releasing full control while still holding true to yourself. Sway side to side. Let the rhythm connect with the bonfire.

10. A sweat may break out. When it grows too hot on your skin, or you get a rush of cold air, step back and sit down. Contemplate what you experienced and ground yourself in the present.

Middle Campfire Scrying

Campfires and other middle-sized outdoor flames can be used for beginners wishing to scry. Though less potent, their heat radiates enough to warm the sense and mask preconceived notions. A healthy fire produces healthy results.

MATERIALS NEEDED: Wine, water, or natural enhancer (if desired); fire, self, three sticks

TO PREPARE: Build a good-sized fire.

THE WORK:

1. Collect three sticks and go kneel before the flames. Drink wine, water, or make use of other natural enhancers.

2. Hold one sick before the fire. Meditate on physical sensations—how the fire warms the skin and the stick is hard in one's palm. Lay it before the fire.

3. Hold the second stick up to the fire. Meditate on how it affects the mind, how the act of building a fire creates a sense of accomplishment and the stick feeds the mind new ideas. Lay it before the fire.

4. Hold the third stick out to the fire. Meditate on its ability to become an instrument of direction, on how it can draw the power of fire in or expel energies from the person holding it. Lay it before the fire with the others.

5. Meditate on the flames and how they relate to yourself, your life, and the lives of everyone who has or will ever be.

6. Bow to the fire and grab the sticks. Throw them into the fire one by one to deepen your relationship with this particular blaze.

7. Dance around the blaze. Sing, laugh. Release all pent-up energies.

8. Find a welcoming spot before the fire and sit in a comfortable position.

9. Clear the mind and look to the flames. Stare at the outlines of each dancing spark. Study the bright light reaching up into the sky. Follow the smoke, ash, and embers as they are released above.

10. Gaze back down the flames to the central source. Find the blue or green heat that glows brightest. That is the most potent aspect of the fire. If no blue-green flames are seen, keep focused on the centermost part of the fire.

11. Breathe deep. Become conscious of your breathing and its relation to the flames. They hiss and sizzle. They need air to breathe as well. Inhale in time with that. Give yourself time to develop a sense of how the flames live.

12. Now relax the eyes. Keep looking at the fire, but defocus the eyes. Instead of seeking definition and contrast let the mind wander as it will, but remain conscious of your breathing and the heat before you.

13. Do the flames say anything? Are there pictures forming in the light? Lean forward. Rock back and forth to help keep with the rhythm of the bonfire.

14. Let the fire take hold of you until the body is exhausted. Then lie back and ground yourself by focusing on the grasses and dirt beneath you.

Small Outdoor Scrying

Small outdoor fires are tricky. They do not "speak" as loud as other, larger fires. Because of this, they require more of a purpose: a mother looking out for the well-being of her child or a concerned brother looking to watch over his sibling. These kinds of bonds draw more power from people. They do not need dire circumstances to be found, and the more versed someone is in this art, the better they can read the flames, but approaching small fire scrying in the right light creates a more successful path.

MATERIALS NEEDED: Wine, water, or natural enhancer (if desired); fire, self, handful of twigs

TO PREPARE: Build a good-sized fire.

THE WORK:

1. Collect handful of twigs and go sit before the flames. Drink wine, water, or make use of other natural enhancers.

2. Hold the twigs out to the fire. Close your eyes and meditate on the wood warming. Visualize each twig as a truth waiting to be uncovered.

3. Meditate on the flames and how they reveal the truth no matter how painful or damning it may be.

4. Bow to the twigs, then look to the fire. Ready the mind for untainted answers. Prepare the body and the higher self for the impacts they may receive.

5. Now stand and throw the twigs into the fire. Drink more wine, water, or use natural enhancers here.

6. Sing or chant and walk around the fire. Step in time and speed the pace until moved to dance with the rhythm of the fire's changing light.

7. Find a welcoming spot and sit in a comfortable position before the flames.

8. Clear the mind and look to a specific spark. Stare at the center of one single flame while the others burn along beside it. Though populations burn in one great haze each person is their own flame. Let the flame represent you and your place within the great work of life.

9. Breathe deep. Inhale as the flame breathes, exhale as it consumes more wood.

10. Relax the body. Expand the mind and your energies within. Stay focused on your flame. Ask it questions. Whether in the mind, through song,

chant, or whisper, your words should match the nature of the flame and the space containing it. Direct specific concerns and listen.

11. Let the fire take hold of you until the body is exhausted. Then lie back and ground yourself by focusing on the grasses and dirt beneath you.

Indoor/Fireplace Scrying

Indoor scrying is highly based on an individual's connection to their living space. The more comfortable a person is performing this rite within that area, the more successful it will be.

It is vital to approach this smaller scale and more potent aspect of seeing beyond time with respect, trust, and confidence. Achieving a heightened sense of being through meditation and previously performed spells furthers this process.

This rite is more difficult than other forms of scrying but also more revealing once properly understood and practiced. Whether incorporating it into ritual or before or after a celebration or event, the lessons learned from opening the mind to broader prospects enlightens those who are ready to connect to something beyond themselves.

MATERIALS NEEDED: Wine, water, or natural enhancer (if desired); fireplace, fire, self, timepiece (watch, hourglass, clock, etc.)

TO PREPARE: Take a walk outside and collect a few natural items for decorating a hearth or altar. Bless the wine, water, or other enhancers by dipping fingers into cup of it or along container and focusing your energies on pouring your power into it. Build a good-sized fire.

THE WORK:

1. Set up the hearth or an altar before the fireplace or wood burning stove. Place symbols of the season along it, as well as the timepiece.

2. Bow before the flames and kneel in front of the timepiece. Take a sip of wine or water, or a small amount of natural enhancer.

3. Close your eyes and place hands on it. Meditate on the meaning of keeping time. How it measures lives and existence, the emphasis it puts on schedules, memories, and humanity's perception of the future.

4. Look to the fire. Sip more wine or water, or take another portion of natural enhancer, and hold the timepiece up to it. Whisper, chant,

sing, or shout words to connect time with flame. Speak of how the ultimate timekeeper is the sun and our planet's positioning.

5. Place the timepiece back in its spot for the rite and lean forward. Sip more wine or water, or take another portion of natural enhancer. Raise hands out to the fire. Close your eyes. Meditate on the warmth of reality. How what is experienced is the test of time. All aspects of being will someday drift beyond the present. Nothing is consistent because time is not just a measurement but a force—one humanity has yet to fully understand.

6. Open your eyes. Stare into the flames, leaving behind physical constraints. Look over each flame. See it twist and twirl in pure freedom. Watch this dance until your eyes become heavy or relaxed. As you fall into the trance direct your focus to the heat at the center of the fire. Peer upon it with curiosity and selflessness.

7. Send out energies asking to be educated, not answered. Images, words, or sensations will reach toward you and consume your thoughts. Give yourself up to them. Forget your surroundings until your body calls you back with discomfort.

8. Stiffness, sweat, or chills will remind you of yourself. When finished, scoot back and lie down on the floor. Contemplate what you experienced and relax.

9. Clear the mind and ground yourself by stretching your limbs and letting your energies neutralize through the floor.

Single Flame/Candle Scrying

Candles host a certain air. A single flame may not burn very hot, but it has the power to grow into an unstoppable fire. It is the potential, the possibilities that spark from this source. That is what makes a candle so perfect for scrying.

Wisdom and skill are what drives this practice. Without the proper knowledge and experience, candle scrying is lost upon the conductor of this symphonic light.

One must never rush into a process of this magnitude. It combines meditation, spellwork, faith, and existence with more than the average person is capable of handling. When readied in this level of magic, a person is met with a web of connections that spring from simple truths and universal answers.

MATERIALS NEEDED: Wine, water, or natural enhancer (if desired); fireplace, fire, self, timepiece (watch, hourglass, clock, etc.)

TO PREPARE: Take a walk outside and collect a few natural items to decorate hearth or altar with. Bless the wine, water, or other enhancers by dipping fingers into cup of it or along container and focusing your energies on pouring your power into it.

THE WORK:

1. Set an altar with symbols of the season, a drink and/or other natural enhancer, candles to represent the god(s)/powers that be/the universe (facing north), a timepiece, and the specific scrying candle.

2. Take a sip of wine or water, or a small amount of natural enhancer. Light all the candles but the scrying one. Bow to the hourglass.

3. Close your eyes and place your hands on the hourglass. Meditate on the meaning of keeping time, how it measures lives and existence, the emphasis it puts on schedules, memories, and humanity's perception of the future.

4. Open your eyes. Sit tall and sip more wine or water, or take another portion of natural enhancer. Gaze between the timepiece and the candle. Light the scrying candle while whispering, chanting, singing, or shouting words to connect time with flame. Speak of reaching out to the sun and our planet's positioning through this rite.

5. Sip more wine or water, or take another portion of natural enhancer. Hold hand over the scrying flame. Close your eyes. Meditate on the warmth of reality, how what is experienced is the test of time. All aspects of being will someday drift beyond the present. Nothing is consistent because time is not just a measurement but a force—one humanity has yet to fully understand.

6. Open your eyes. Stare at the flame. Leave behind physical constraints. Watch how the small spark moves or holds position. Appreciate the

beauty in its posture and focus on the glow until your eyes become heavy or relaxed.

7. As you fall into the trance, focus your energies on combining your mind and spirit with the flame. Visualize yourself within that great element, living without fear or mortality. Images, words, or sensations will consume you. Let them take over.

8. Forget yourself until discomfort calls you back to your body. Stiffness, sweat, or chills will remind you of yourself. When awakened bow to the flame. Scoot back and lie down on the floor. Contemplate what you experienced and relax.

9. Clear the mind and ground yourself by stretching your limbs and feeling the air caress the skin above while the floor neutralizes your energies from below.

Spells

When choosing to influence the powers that be, a person must take full consideration and be realistic about the purpose of the work. Spells can save lives and have the ability to help and heal. They can also punish or teach lessons to individuals who refuse to listen to reason. No matter what the intention, the absolute truth of the matter will come through and reflect on everyone involved—especially the caster.

Fire spells are incredibly active. They do not rest until the end is met. They move quickly, burning through whatever fuel is available. To properly make use of this great energy, meditation must be mastered and the balance between logic and emotion upheld. When cast in the right light, fire spells make the world glow.

FIRE SPELL TO RESOLVE AN ISSUE

Materials Needed: Self, candle or fire materials, pen and paper (firesafe bowl if using a candle)

To Prepare: Wait until new moon or waning moon to perform.

THE WORK:

1. Build a fire or light a candle and sit before the flame(s).

2. Write down the issue that is weighing down your being.

3. Cup the paper in both hands. Close your eyes. Meditate on it and its meaning. Focus your energies on the power you have given to it.

4. Now hold the paper over the flame(s)—make sure to have a firesafe bowl to burn the paper in if using candle. Visualize the paper and the issues as the same being. Now light it with the candle and place in bowl to burn, or drop into the fire.

5. Give yourself closure even if no one else will.

6. Watch the flames until the paper is completely destroyed. Then lie back and focus on the present. Leave the past behind.

FIRE SPELL TO BANISH ILL WILL

MATERIALS NEEDED: Self, fire, three pieces of string

TO PREPARE: Build a fire on a full moon or waning moon.

THE WORK:

1. Stand before the fire and clear the mind.

2. Take up a piece of string. Let it represent you or the person running from negativity. Close your eyes and visualize it as that person, pouring energy into it until it truly feels connected to the subject of the spell. Set it before the fire.

3. Take up the second piece of string. Let it represent the person interfering with the subject. Close your eyes and see it as that person. Pour energies into the string until it is fully charged to represent the interloper. Say their name. Chant it, sing it; shout it as needed. Set it before the fire next to the first piece.

4. Take up the third piece of string. This is negative connection the subject has to the antagonist. Now grab the first two strings and wrap this third one around them. Feel its power.

5. Chant, sing, whisper, or yell words to release the subject from this harm. Hold the strings up to the sky, then dangle them over the flames.

6. Drop the strings into the flames and walk around the fire focusing on banishing the unhealthy link between the people. Whisper, chant, sing, or dance for this purpose.

7. When the flames die down stop. Stand before the fire. Gaze down where the strings once were and nod. So mote it be.

FIRE SPELL TO PROTECT A LOVED ONE OR SELF

MATERIALS NEEDED: Self, fire, picture of loved one or self (a drawing or photo)

TO PREPARE: Build a fire on a waxing moon, or full moon.

THE WORK:

1. Place picture before the fire.

2. Sit in front of the picture facing the fire. Clear the mind.

3. Look to the loved one or picture of self. Fixate on the being captured in the image—the spirit, the personality.

4. Now gaze upon the flames. Move in close and feel the heat of their protective energies.

5. Hold the picture up to the fire. Focus on the image as it illuminates. Visualize the person being engulfed in the warmth of safety. Then whisper, chant, or sing words to seal this rite asking the fire to look after the subject.

6. Then offer the image up to the flames in exchange for the fire's security. As it burns turn the mind toward the life and vitality of the person being preserved and protected.

7. When the flames die down sit back and ground the self in reality.

FIRE SPELL TO OPEN THE MIND

MATERIALS NEEDED: Self, fire materials

TO PREPARE: Take a purification bath and meditate to clear the mind.

The Work:

1. Build a fire or light a candle and stand before the flame(s).

2. Watch the fire dance. See how it consumes the wood and absorbs its energy to burn brighter.

3. Hold your hands over the fire. Let the warmth heat the body starting at the fingertips and moving inward.

4. When the mind is warmed, press fingertips to the forehead. Visualize thought and knowledge as fuel and your brain as the fire that consumes it to give off more brilliance. Set aside dividing lines, political bias, religious boundaries, and racial or cultural bonds.

5. The flames rage against whatever stands in their way. But unlike humans, the element is not susceptible to misinformation, misdirection, or martial tactics. Ponder this.

6. Raise hands up to the sky. Imagine sitting with those who disagree with you and reaching an understanding. See yourself reaching beyond your being and discovering truths, energies, and powers unknown to society.

7. Bring hands back over the fire and relate that to others. Instead of letting the idea drive ego, find humility in the knowledge that everyone can attain a higher being if they work hard enough. Be humbled by your role in the universe and seek out the best way to carry it through.

8. Chant, sing, whisper, or yell words to seal the quest for untainted enlightenment. Fully dedicate the self to the pursuit of happiness not just for your being, but those around you and beyond.

9. Kneel before the fire and ground yourself with the earth beneath you. Relax your energies and let the present welcome you back.

FIRE SPELL TO HEAL WOUNDS

Materials Needed: Self or person who is ailing, fire materials, one rock or quartz rock for each issue

To prepare: Take a purification bath and meditate to prepare the mind.

THE WORK:

1. Build a fire and place the rock(s) along it to heat up.

2. Walk around the fire and focus the mind on healing whatever ails the body, thoughts, or being.

3. Sit before the rocks facing the fire. Make sure to be close enough to feel the force of the heat, but far enough away to avoid scorching the skin.

4. Now take up the rock (or first one). Hold it over the area of the body having issues, the head (for mental issues), or the chest (for spiritual issues).

5. Chant, whisper, or sing words to heal.

6. Press the rock to the skin where the physical problem is on self or other person, the forehead (for mental issues), or the chest (for spiritual issues).

7. Close your eyes and visualize the heat being absorbed into the area that needs tending. See the pain subsiding to the power of the fire. Focus on mending whatever needs fixing. Let the heat guide the spell.

8. It may inspire you to rub the physical ailment, rock back and forth, or dance before the fire. It all depends on the need. Listen to the energies and let them guide the work.

9. Repeat for multiple ailments.

10. When the rock(s) cool, meditate on the purpose. Then clear the mind and ground the self.

FIRE SPELL FOR SELF-LOVE

MATERIALS NEEDED: Self, candle or fire materials, pen and paper (firesafe bowl if using a candle)

TO PREPARE: Take a purification bath. Build a fire or light a candle in readied space.

THE WORK:

1. Stand before the flame. Look down on the light.

2. Close your eyes. Visualize yourself standing in the glow. Think of what you wish the light to reach and what aspects of yourself you long to keep in the darkness.

3. Stare at the flame and kneel. Eye every possible area of your body. Think of all the aspects that make up your mind. Search your soul for bits of perfection as well as flaws.

4. Sit on your bottom and take up the pen and paper. Hold it to the light. Whisper, chant, or sing words of acceptance and love.

5. On one side write out all the worst aspects of who you are. On the other write out the best.

6. Hold the paper up to the light again. See yourself for who you truly are. Did you leave anything out? Whether it is written or not, everything will come out. Be honest with yourself and put it all down on the paper.

7. Now look at what you wish to improve—bad habits, defects, negativities. Cross out the elements of yourself you wish to change or be rid of.

8. Then look at what makes you proud of yourself. Run your fingers over your greatest accomplishments and traits. Hug them close.

9. Stand up once more and hold the paper above the flames. Chant, sing, whisper, or shout words of accepting yourself as you are but always striving to improve and be at your best.

10. Place the paper in the fire to burn, or ignite with candle flame and drop in the firesafe bowl.

11. Focus on this purpose until the fire dies down. Then sit back and meditate, grounding the self back in the present.

7
TREES

Sitting within a veil of leaves, hiding in the embrace of knobby branches: these comforts remain a viable source of strength and remedy. Within the comforts of a tree, I am more equipped to look beyond the stress of modern life. Instead of getting swept up in mindlessness, something about tree climbing or just sitting in a tree offers perspective.

Climbing upward is the perfect analogy for life. Most people wish to keep moving upward. We start from the bottom and strive to achieve harder and harder accomplishments until we have reached a secure spot that suits us.

There are those who seek knowledge from the act of climbing. The knowledge born from experience, failure, and repeated attempts, and that which comes with effort and persistence is all present when conquering the heights that trees sprout along. Whether for physical, academic, or higher reasons, tree climbing offers new opportunities to reach beyond the self and perform spells that tangle through the twigs surrounding a person.

One doesn't have to literally climb a tree to experience this natural high. Do not put yourself in danger if you are not confident or able/equipped. Plenty of bushes or low-lying trees provide a new vantage point that allows us to see through the leaves or rest among branches with our feet securely planted on the ground if afraid of heights or unable/unwilling to climb.

From low-lying structures with simple ground level bases to the elaborate constructs resembling childhood fancy, tree houses warm the spirit while offering shelter and a reprieve from the boxy houses and blocky construction that has consumed architecture. One can even create their own structure with minimal materials if all that's wanted is a nice landing at the base of a tree. Regardless of how it stands, staying in a tree house allows one to enjoy recreational activities like drawing, music, writing, painting, or crafts with a new aspect. Within that space is a different kind of energy. It is made for inspiration and creativity.

Tree Stands

Tree climbing isn't just about the leaves and the branches. Those elements do possess their own power and magical properties, but the atmosphere alone gives a person the air of visiting another realm.

When wishing to escape society, or climb up into the skies for longer periods of time, tree stands offer a small floor space. They can have rails or even a small table, but their main purpose is to offer better footing for daily adventures. Instead of climbing into the boughs for an hour or less, a person can spend an entire morning or day among their favorite tree.

With more secure comfort, these structures are suitable for recreation, studying, hunting (for those who engage in this ancient practice), or spellwork.

Tree stand time sets aside the troubles of the world to allow an individual to search themselves and find solutions they can realistically carry out to do their part. Just watching a family of deer creep out into the open or a bird swoop down for food displays cause and effect the way it is—no influence, bias, or control is pressed upon one's perception when they sit on their own floor within a tree. Having the freedom to think and explore ideas undistracted breeds a love of knowledge and understanding. Books are always welcome among the treetops; they are best read where they originated from.

Getting to a tree stand and focusing personal energies on other, more positive thoughts makes life clearer as the day that unfolds beneath. It offers a serene, conscientious alternative.

Then there are the spells that one can perform above the ground. Floor space offers room for simple materials and slight movement. From spells to draw out animals to those that bless a life taken, tree stand spells rely on the power of earth and air to influence surrounding energies.

For Knowledge

The world slows down when my feet are off the ground. "Looking down" lends insight.

Those who seek out the comfort of trees are usually on a journey for meaning and wisdom. Wisdom come over time if a person is perceptive enough to read the symbols laid before them in life. That takes a great deal of knowledge, whether drawn from experience, education, or intuition.

Experience is our first learning method. From the moment a person kicks inside the womb to when they suckle at the breast, everything that happens is a learning experience. The brain memorizes results needed to survive. Even muscles have an ability to "remember" what they have learned through carrying out an act. Singers have a muscle memory for well-practiced songs. Even when plagued with throat illnesses like laryngitis, they can perfectly remember songs that they have sung numerous times.

Magic is the same way. Individuals who are well practiced have a muscle memory that allows the body to build energy even on the roughest days. It encourages the brain to focus no matter what distractions are presented. The spirit expands and reaches out based on how well versed a person is.

In a tree stand, all of those instincts are elevated (whether the "stand" is at the base of a tree on the ground or among the clouds). Getting closer to the skies is attained through a direct focus on the trees and their tallest reach; they automatically set a scene. And in that scene, thoughts turn toward more meaningful matters.

People can engage in activities anywhere, but among the arms of a tree an individual's instinctual self comes back out. It swings around and observes the area with greater ability. Instead of fearing the unknown, the knowledge is more easily embraced.

Trees do not know when they will fall. They rock and sway to ensure longevity, but that does not ensure safety. Connecting to this internal link that reminds humans that we will die, but we also have the ability to live as we need until that time comes, enhances meditations, prepares hunters for their work, and aids spells.

Tree stand meditations combine experience with education and intuition. They bring it all forward and make way for a new understanding.

To perform:

1. Go to the tree stand/base of the tree.

2. Stand and look out upon the earth below.

3. Close your eyes and let go of your roots. Be free. Let your energies run wild with the wind.

4. Kneel and place hands on thighs. Visualize yourself in truth, as you are entirely. Think of how that relates to other truths in the world. The absolute ones, mind you: ties to others, ties to obligations, objects, skills, and tasks.

5. Now sit back. Contemplate what you know. Respect that everything you know is based on either intuition, experience, or education. Meditate on the foundation of learning. Why is it important? How is it better spread? What could be done to share it better?

6. Listen to the tree. Be perceptive to the wind. Draw on the energies and powers above and below to take yourself and your purpose further.

7. When the body is exhausted, lie back or sit comfortably. Breathe deep and look out once more. Place palms on the floor and balance your energies. Further grounding may be wise once you have climbed out of the tree stand.

Tree Houses

Many animals make their homes among the trees. Various birds, squirrels, and other creatures know the shelter of branch and bark. Like the creatures in the wild, children relate to this freedom. They are more instinctual, less indoctrinated by society.

Humans in general do not often live among the treetops but we do build tree houses for our kids to enjoy or reach for new heights like our wooden friends. Tree house campsites, retreats, and even hotels have become more common as modernity leaves individuals hungry for natural escapes. When these are not available, the simple bonds of touching a tree and visualizing a home in their branches brings about new energy while keeping our feet on the ground.

Tree houses represent childhood. They bring back memories of being a kid again. That inner child reemerges and releases those energies that pay more attention to the little moments taken for granted.

No one can ever fully leave their world behind. Responsibilities wait for us or find others to tend to the need. A brief pause allows the weight of the tasks and issues to lessen and rejuvenates a person to better meet their obligations. Meditations and spellwork can be performed to help with this. Houses built or envisioned in the trees were made for meditation. They provide a sound structure and the privacy many require to cast strong spells with confidence. The energies sent out during these rites grow within the space they are birthed in and expand far beyond the perimeter based on the practitioner's dedication.

Any or all aspects of staying in a tree house enrich one's life. It takes people back to their roots while lifting them above that which they already know. Tree houses truly are a sanctuary.

For Escape

Talk of escapism is everywhere. Society has led people to see books, music, all forms of entertainment as avenues of escape. There is merit to this; when frivolity rules, people feel it. They become conscious of the emptiness that accumulates. Instead of attacking that emptiness and combating an entire way of living—something foisted upon them—distractions become a source of comfort.

But the consumptive kind of escape is not the same kind as found in a tree house. It is not a place to pretend that nothing is wrong; it is an area that presents the better aspects of life. Instead of pulling focus from life's pressures and negativities, time in a tree house creates for a person a positive environment that fosters new thoughts or rekindles old hopes and ideas.

A tree house will allow a person to escape their former self and draw forth their higher meaning, not escape life. Connecting with the divine and/or the energies of the universe is easier in this space because it provides the comfort of simplicity with the luxury of security. Meditation is carried out more easily in this setting.

To meditate to escape cynicism, frustration, pain, or hatred that sometimes festers in modern society:

1. Sit before the window or open door of the tree house/base of the tree where you can look out.
2. Look to the branches. Watch them sway in the breeze or move under their own weight and the weight of tree creatures. Feel the energy

surrounding them and how that energy accumulates to produce an air of light and purity.

3. Close your eyes. Visualize your daily life. Think of the tasks that are performed regularly. What kind of energy do they foster in you? Is it light and pure or does it drag down your spirits?

4. See yourself approaching these things with a new energy. Envision the air of the tree surrounding you so that you are better able to handle the weight when feeling stepped upon.

5. Open your eyes and focus on the sky beyond the tree.

6. Let your inner power grow and grow until it reaches that height. Feel it surround you and everything surrounding you. Bow and lie back ready to put this new energy into all aspects of life to escape imbalance and discontentment.

Spells

Because trees provide life for humanity, they host special powers that increase personal energies. Traveling to a tree house for recreation or allowing the mind to explore the possibilities makes a person whole, but casting spells in them sends that sense of being beyond the individual.

Venturing to a new space to cast a spell breaks free of routine. It forces us to step away from known comforts to trust in the elements. In doing so, the aura is unique to the trip. Weaving webs within trees is a perfect setting. The elements are fresh and ready. Creatures are called to the area or repelled depending on need. Regardless of the time of year or what the weather has to offer, tree climbing spells require leadership.

For those wishing to discover their true calling, it is never advised to rush into spellwork. Approached in this way, spellwork becomes little more than a passing fad, something to later be taken for granted and used for mindless tasks that could easily be resolved with hard work and patience.

Casting a spell while "climbing a tree" is risky, whether physically climbing or not, because of the power that trees host. Doing both requires a full connection between the physical, mental, spiritual, and eternal (nature continues to. exist with or without humanity) stages of being.

When I feel the need to take on this difficult task, it calls to me. It is as if the trees are speaking directly to my spirit, and the urge writhes within. My instincts speak out and demand that I listen and I find new opportunities opening up to me if and when I make the time to respond to this tug.

The following spells are meant for avid tree climbers who have practiced the art of knowing themselves and reached out to the world around them with multiple talents or techniques.

CONIFEROUS CLIMBING SPELL

MATERIALS NEEDED: Large healthy evergreen tree, self, pine needles/pine cone(s)

TO PREPARE: Wear clothing with pockets or carry a very small satchel or bag attached to wrist

THE WORK:

1. Approach tree and find the best route to start climbing, whether literally or through meditation is a personal decision one must make. Grasp branches with hands and balance the feet. Balance the use of both arms and legs.

2. Get at least five to ten feet off the ground. Now sit on a sturdy branch. Look out at the surrounding area. Breathe in the pine-scented air.

3. Focus on the branches closest to you. Balance yourself and grasp the nearest bough with needles. Make sure your body is secure but shake the pine needles into other hand or in lap. Place a few into pocket or satchel.

4. Climb another ten feet or more. Again, stop and sit down. Balance and grasp the nearest bough with pine cones or needles. Shake a few free to pocket or place in satchel.

5. Repeat as comfort allows or until reaching the top of the tree.

6. When at the highest point of the climb, secure self in comfortable position (can be sitting, kneeling, or standing).

7. Take the pine cone(s) and/or needles out and hold them before your eyes in one hand. Meditate on them. Visualize their natural energy and how it aids you on your journey.

8. Now envision these tokens of the tree you are visiting drawing your instincts forth, bringing them out of hiding. What do they say? How do they guide you? Listen and learn. Be willing to take your time.

9. With each reveal thank the tree and drop one or more of the needles to the ground. When only pine cones are left pocket them or place in satchel and climb down.

10. From the foot of the tree, sit among the roots. Place the pine cone(s) against the grounded veins of the tree, making sure that they touch the root.

11. Bow your head and whisper, sing, or chant about starting and finishing being connected. Think of how every beginning in your life affects each success or end. Look for truths, patterns, hidden in past enterprises. Now turn the mind to new budding opportunities and how those patterns, beginnings and ends can influence better approaches.

12. Breathe deep and lie down underneath or beside the tree to ground the self.

DECIDUOUS CLIMBING SPELL

Materials Needed: Large leafy tree (oak, maple, etc.), self

To Prepare: Wear clothing with pockets or carry a very small satchel or bag attached to wrist. Climb in spring, summer, or fall.

The Work:

1. Approach tree and find the best route to start climbing (again visualization is the best substitute if preferred). Grasp branches with your hands and balance your feet. Balance the use of both arms and legs.

2. Get at least ten to fifteen feet off the ground. Balance self and look out. Breathe in the fresh air. Look through the twigs and leaves.

3. Focus on the branches closest to you. Meditate on it. Visualize the natural energy and the power it contains.

4. Balance yourself and grasp the bough. Pool your energies and push them out onto the branch. Feel that extension of yourself spread through the limb and into the twigs and leaves at the furthest reaches. Now shake

the branch and experience the jolt. Trust yourself and the tree to remain standing even if a few leaves should fall or twigs break off.

5. Again climb ten feet or more. Stop and stand or even crouch at the new height. Gaze out beyond. Study the scenery. Then slowly pull focus back to the leaves and/or twigs closest to you. Meditate on the new branch; visualize the energies radiating from it and its components like before.

6. Rebalance and grasp the branch, spreading your personal power until it extends through that area of the tree. Shake the branch and revel in the sensation of survival and perseverance.

7. Repeat as comfort allows or until reaching the top of the tree.

8. Reach the top or highest point of comfort and stand tall. Gaze down. See the height you have achieved. Whisper, chant, or sing your thanks to the tree for sharing its strength.

9. Now climb down, taking care along the way.

10. From the foot of the tree, place hands along the trunk and gaze up.

11. Bow head and whisper, sing, or chant of the power in a strong foundation. Think of how all successes come from strong passions, or desires that mean the most to you. Look to the past and see yourself as a sapling learning to withstand the elements. Now turn the mind to where you stand now. What are your passions rooted in? How do they grow? Is there anything you can do to strengthen the bonds between yourself and this endeavor so it climbs higher?

12. Listen to the tree. Listen to your instincts. Follow the answers like they are branches to be climbed.

13. Sit down and breathe deep. Touch the ground and focus on balancing your energies.

LIGHTENING THE MOOD

(When struggling to relax and enjoy life)

Materials Needed: Tree stand/base of tree, self, candle and matches or other light source

To Prepare: Go to tree stand/base of tree with candle and matches or other light source.

The Work:

1. Sit comfortably before the candle or light source.

2. Look up to the sky and around to the tree that supports you. Light or illuminate your light source.

3. Cup hands around the brilliance. Close your eyes. Feel the warmth against your skin. Draw the warmth inside you.

4. Search for the passion and heat within where happiness sparks. Recall treasured memories.

5. Now open eyes. Gaze upon the candle or light. Clear the mind and watch the flame dance.

6. Meditate on what is blocking your ability to find joy. Relationships, jobs, home life, or other issues can present many problems. Look at the issue from every angle. Even in dire circumstances laughter and love still exist—if they didn't, people would not survive tragedy, poverty, war, or other painful aspects of life.

7. Build your energies off of the heat from the candle. Let them grow beyond yourself. Visualize solutions or compromises that will ease frustration.

8. Stare at the candle or light. See it as the obstacles weighing down the issue. Extinguish the flame while chanting words of overcoming the struggle.

9. Sit back and look to the sky once more. Gaze around the branches nearby and let their simplicity ground you.

CONVERSING WITH THE FIELDS

(Must be done near a field space)

Materials Needed: Tree stand or base of tree, self, container of water

To Prepare: Go to tree stand/base of tree with the container of water.

THE WORK:

1. Sit comfortably before the container of water.

2. Look to the field. Clear the mind and meditate on what you see. Really examine the grasses, any bare patches, or animals within sight. Let it reveal what it may.

3. Close your eyes. If using a small container, dip a single finger into the water, if bigger, dig all your fingers in. Visualize how waters slip through fields. They form above and watch all that unfolds before raining down and being absorbed below. Focus on what they learn along the way.

4. Follow the images or sounds/words that appear in the mind. Let the droplets guide you.

5. Then open your eyes and bow to the water. Flick small amounts or handfuls of water down to the ground below as an offering. Thank the water for speaking to your energies.

6. Drink one sip of the water to ground the body. Relax.

READING A FOREST

(Must be done in a tree stand which is near a forest or in sight of one)

MATERIALS NEEDED: Tree stand or base of tree, self

TO PREPARE: Go to tree stand/base and sit comfortably.

THE WORK:

1. Breathe deep. Look out to the forest. Scan the trees until your eye is drawn to a specific area.

2. Focus on that spot. Watch it. Meditate on it. Is it a large space, or a single bush or leaf?

3. Feel the energy of that area. Close your eyes and keep the image in your mind. Whisper, sing, or chant to it.

4. Now push your personal energies closer to that corner of the forest. Really reach out. Listen. Be perceptive to your inner voice. Let your instincts guide you. Images, sounds, or words may come to mind. Ponder them and their connection to you and your purpose.

5. Open eyes and repeat as many times as you wish.

6. When finished stand and extend arms up to the sky, then down to your toes. Let the stretches recall you to your own consciousness and ground it to the body. Then reflect on what was experienced.

DRAWING AN ANIMAL FORTH

MATERIALS NEEDED: Tree stand or base of tree, self, snack (e.g., a piece of bread, fruit, or vegetable), and a piece of rope, yarn, or string

TO PREPARE: Go to tree stand or base of tree with items.

THE WORK:

1. Sit comfortably before the food and string.

2. Look up to the sky, then down to the floor and speak words of balance and trust between all living beings.

3. Now scan the world around you. Think of whether you wish to see a specific animal or not. If wishing to draw out a specific creature, visualize them in your mind. Hold that image and do not let go, even when performing the rest of the spell. If more relaxed in what you wish to see, visualize all the woodland creatures you can imagine and focus on that idea all throughout the spell.

4. Take up the food. While focusing on the animal(s), draw out your inner savage, the wild part of yourself that craves sustenance. Envision how food brings all beings together. How it forges deeper relationships, and seals love and trust between humans and the animals they live among. Set the food back down.

5. Still focusing on the animal(s), take up the string or rope. Feel how it can be used for positive or negative purposes, to divide or bring together. Wrap the string around your food item. Tie it tight and hang it among the branches of the tree. Let it represent your offering, the sacrifices you are willing to make in order to reach out to other creatures. Whisper, chant, or sing of this purpose as you finishing tying it up.

6. Sit back down and bow your head. Meditate on your purpose quietly. Then open your eyes and observe nature until a wild friend is revealed.

7. Do NOT cast this spell for hunting purposes. That is not its intent. Respect the process and let the result ground you.

MAKING PROPER CHOICES

Materials Needed: Tree stand or base of tree, self, coin

To Prepare: Go to the tree stand or the base of tree with the coin.

The Work:

1. Sit comfortably and take out the coin.

2. Set it in front of you. Meditate on it to represent the negative and positive repercussions of our actions.

3. Now hold coin between thumb and forefinger. Close your eyes.

4. Think of the issue you are torn on. See it in its full potential. How can it affect you and others?

5. Now hold the coin up to the sky. Look at it beneath the heavens. See the size in relation to the expanse above. No matter how great a choice may seem, it is much smaller in the endless work of the universe. Let that comfort you and build your energies. Find confidence in the truth that whatever you decide, the changes resulting from it will find balance eventually.

6. Stand up. Roll the coin along the nearest branch, back and forth as many times as needed. As it spins meditate on your purpose and what best suits it. Listen to the tree as its bark whispers back. Feel the pull of the higher self, leading you toward the most balanced choice.

7. Let go of selfishness and useless want. Seek the need. That is where the answer lies. Far too often wants suppress needs. They spoil and tarnish.

8. Whisper, chant, or sing of the decision and be free in a solid declaration.

9. Toss the coin below. Climb to the ground in search of it. When you do find it, you will be grounded and set on your path.

TO PLAY WITH YOUR INNER CHILD

MATERIALS NEEDED: Tree house or base of tree, self, mirror, toy

TO PREPARE: Take a purification bath if inclined. Go into a tree house or to the base of tree with your materials. Set the toy on top of the mirror in the center of the room.

THE WORK:

1. Walk around the inside of the tree house/base of tree in a circle one way, then another. Clap and sing old nursery rhyme(s) as you do so.

2. Smile and laugh at yourself. Then go to the mirror and kneel before the toy. Recall how you played with it and what it meant to you when you were young. (If you do not have a toy from your childhood then obtain one and think of what it represents to all children, how it would make you feel if you were a child again.)

3. Pick it up and play with it. Don't concern yourself with time or what others would think. Just enjoy the moment as you enjoyed playing in your youth.

4. Now take up the mirror. Hold it so you can see yourself and the toy. Study your features. Your forehead, eyes, nose, cheeks, mouth, and chin have changed over the years.

5. Now close your eyes. Visualize yourself when you were young. See the image staring back as it did when you brushed your teeth or looked at yourself in the mirror as a child. Focus on the details of your forehead, eyes, nose, cheeks, mouth, and chin. See the sparkling light in your eyes. Find that warm glow upon your cheeks.

6. Open your eyes and look for the child that was. See it in the eyes and skin.

7. Whisper, chant, or sing words of remembering silliness, carefree and happy times, and how you can still enjoy them like you did when the world was new to you.

8. Get back up and dance or clap around the room with the toy. Let it serve as a conductor, a generator for whimsical energies.

9. When exhausted, lie down and take a nap as you did in those years before responsibility and obligation took over completely.

BUILDING BLESSING

Materials Needed: Tree house or base of tree, self, candle and matches, sage, small bowl of salt and bowl of water

To Prepare: Take a purification bath if inclined. Then bless the water and salt by individually touching each and pouring your energies into them.

The Work:

1. Approach the tree house or base of tree with candles, sage, bowls of salt and water.

2. Walk around the tree house/base, underneath/on the ground. Chant, whisper, or sing words of blessing the land, the materials that sprang from the god(s)/universe by the powers of earth, air, fire, and water. Then take up bowl of salt and walk around sprinkling a ring of salt beneath. Turn in the opposite direction, take up bowl of water, and walk around sprinkling water on ground in a circle.

3. Now light the sage and cleanse the area by walking a circle with the sage.

4. Carry materials up into tree house and set the candle in the center of the room with the matches and sage.

5. Again, walk in a circle around the room casting a circle by chanting, singing, or whispering words of blessings from the god(s)/universe by the powers of earth, air, fire, and water. Do so with salt and then turn and go the opposite way with the water.

6. Once more, light the sage and cleanse the area by walking a circle with the sage.

7. When ready, stand before the candle at the center of the room. Hold the sage in non-dominant hand and raise arms upward (without touching the roof). Call upon the forces as above and so below, then reach down.

8. Light the candle and sit before it. Meditate on making this space as warm as the flame but as cool and changing as the outer wax.

9. Stand once more and go before each wall, facing it. Spread your arms out and speak your blessing, using words that invite the gods/universe, the elements, and all respectful beings in with love.

10. Dance around the candle or sing before it. Let the energies build and rise from within. Then bow to the candle. So mote it be.

CALLING UPON OTHERS

MATERIALS NEEDED: Tree house or base of tree, self, paper or a community newsletter

TO PREPARE: Take a purification bath if inclined. Go into tree house or base of tree with the paper. (If you cannot find a community newsletter, write a note to yourself about your community—what is missing and what helps the people come together.)

THE WORK:

1. Place the paper in the center of the space.

2. Sit before it.

3. Place right hand on left shoulder and left hand on right shoulder. Put your chin to your chest and close your eyes. Meditate on yourself and your role in your neighborhood. How you interact or don't interact with others.

4. Relax and place hands at your sides. Open your eyes and look straight ahead. Chant words of togetherness, building lasting friendships/alliances that benefit everyone.

5. Look to the paper. Meditate on it. Visualize neighbors and others reaching out to you, being more communicative.

6. Grab the paper and hold it up. Chant again, the same words of togetherness and community as before but with the energies drawn forth from the instinct to accept your neighbors as friends and family.

7. Do so until the body is exhausted. Then lie back and breathe deep. Ground yourself and prepare for new encounters.

FINDING VALUE IN DIFFERING TRUTHS

MATERIALS NEEDED: Tree house or base of tree, self

TO PREPARE: Take a purification bath.

THE WORK:

1. Go to tree house or base of tree and meditate before the window or open door.

2. Close your eyes. Recall disputes, political arguments, workplace issues with coworkers, etc. Go through each, one at a time.

3. Now stand. Raise your arms up to the ceiling. Chant for understanding and the ability to remain calm even when feeling verbally attacked. Find the instinct to look to reason instead of lashing out.

4. Kneel and close your eyes once more. Lean forward and go over each dispute, argument, or issue again one by one, but this time project yourself out of the situation. Let your being float between yourself and the person engaging in opposition.

5. When opposition grows angry or belligerent, it is usually tied to fear or desperation. Think of how that comes through in these situations and work to find the thread that holds their beliefs in place. Respect that even those who do not see your viewpoint may be just as educated and informed as you. Instead of assuming they are ignorant, think of their knowledge and ponder what might be if they are correct.

6. Do the ends align with the information? Does it matter? How do your words and actions matter to the world in relation to theirs when removing the constraints of time and current events?

7. Open your eyes and stand in the doorway of your tree house. Glance down. Look at the distance below. Some truths come from a difference of position. Recognize and apply this to interactions with others.

8. Repeat as needed.

ESCAPING YOUR INNER NAYSAYER

MATERIALS NEEDED: Tree house or base of tree, self, one item you have kept in your home that you do not like (clothes article, food, something; if there aren't any, make or find something you dislike), shovel.

To PREPARE: Place shovel on the ground blow tree house. Bring item up into it.

THE WORK:

1. Place item by the door of the tree house/base of the tree.

2. Sit in the center of the room and meditate. Clear your mind.

3. Visualize how you obtained the item. Was it an impulse purchase? A gift? Why do you keep it?

4. Now think of all the times you doubted yourself, how fear or concerns prevented you from doing what you wanted.

5. Open your eyes and look to the unwanted object. Get up. Stand before it in the doorway. Look down and whisper, chant, or sing words of courage. Speak of better trusting yourself and your instincts.

6. Now push the unwanted item out the door. Watch it fall.

7. Let this act fuel your energies. Grow your personal power. Let it build within until your skin tingles and you cannot resist your inner voice. Let it overpower your doubts and that part of yourself that holds you back.

8. Now climb down/stand on the ground. Look over the object or pieces where it fell. Feel the release of overpowering the naysayer that contradicts your higher being.

9. Grab the shovel and bury the item. As you do so, visualize that you are burying self-consciousness.

10. When finished stand upon the newly moved earth and raise arms to the sky. Call upon the god(s)/universe to aid you in trusting yourself to better listen to your instincts.

COMBATING MODERN PRESSURE

MATERIALS NEEDED: Tree house or base of tree, self, candle and matches

TO PREPARE: Take a purification bath. Bring the materials into tree house.

THE WORK:

1. Place candle in center of space and sit before it facing the door.

2. Light the candle and clear the mind.

3. Close your eyes. Meditate and visualize life pressures that plague you regularly.

4. Open your eyes and focus on the flame before you. Reach forward and hold hands around the flame but not close enough to burn your skin. Feel the heat radiating from it.

5. Absorb that energy. Let it move from your fingers and reach through your entire body. Let it soothe your senses.

6. Now look to the door. Stand and walk around the candle. Place hands on the door frame and press forehead to the door. Whisper, chant, or sing of burning brighter than the tensions that are created by modern society.

7. Open the door and look out. Breathe deep. Stand above your worries and look down on them. Turn your back on the doorway and fixate on the candle's flame. Walk to it and kneel before the light with your back to the door.

8. Whisper, chant, or sing of leaving the stress behind you. Visualize the warmth and energies that exist despite current pressures. Focus on those elements.

9. Bow to the candle and be confident in your purpose.

8
HUNTING, FISHING, FORAGING

No matter how a person lives, the energy to hunt, fish, or forage remains a central aspect of being. They have been such a large part of life for so long that modernity has found contorted ways to implement these principles in society.

Hunting requires so much physical and mental preparation as well as action that when reaching the field and facing a kill, one instantly relies on their instincts. Their spiritual ties reach out and the act reminds them who they really are. In that moment everything becomes clear.

If hunting does not appeal, fishing is another specific action that requires more than superficial modernity. It does not matter how tall or short a person is. The water doesn't care if someone is beautiful or not. Fishing is an act of meditation, a test in patience and respect for nature and one's self. It washes over a person's entire being and calms them for the other aspects of life.

For those unable or unwilling to catch fish or hunt prey, foraging still provides a pleasing practice that engages the body and mind while collecting nourishing foods that bring a person closer to their spiritual self.

However an individual choses to unleash their needs, patience, self-reliance, respect, and mindfulness follow those who approach these different tactics with honor.

Hunting

When looking to the past, society gazes on hunting with a different light. We say, "They *had* to do that to live." It is true that hunting is less of a physical necessity, but for the people who wish to be involved in every aspect of their nutrition and eat meat, hunting isn't about bragging or a thrill; it is a about keeping the age-old wisdom of the hunter's past alive for if and when the time requires it once more.

During the darkest months of the year, meat from fish and game is the most accessible food option if we must fend for ourselves. Our inner voice knows that. It is why many people crave meats and stews during winter.

But it's not just the returns from hunting expeditions that serve our deeper beings. It is the act of setting out and utilizing our knowledge to further our existence. It is the peace of the woods, the anticipation of what the wild has to offer. The chill in the air and the prickling sensations that test patience comprise a special breed of courage not found within more comfortable settings.

Whether using a rifle or bow and arrow, learning to master a weapon and keep it safe until the time comes requires stability and a responsible maturity derived from self-reliance.

When I first went hunting years ago, I discovered confidence in my ability to rely on myself. I realized the transfer of life when I shot a deer and found a deeper respect for the creature that gave its life so that I could live. This also made it easier for me to respect others and all creation. I was already working to care for the planet and habitats in my area, but that instinct grew stronger.

The instinct to hunt manifests in different ways. For the unwise, it manifests in an arrogant manner, but for those more versed in broader aspects of being, it is a blessing that is to be appreciated and adored.

Tracking

There are certain skills born into a human. The thirst for knowledge, exploration, or finding that which we seek lives in everyone. We come from various backgrounds. There is no single approach to building the knowledge needed to track an animal. It just requires logic and reasoning. One must be educated in identifying spoors, scents, and tree rubbings as well as how to mask our own scent, camouflage ourselves, and wait out herds.

Safety education courses are required in many states, I received mine when I was twelve years old. This book learning encouraged me and others to prevent injury or accidental death. Combining what was learned in the classroom with instinctual knowledge and the lessons I gathered from each excursion made me a better tracker.

Someone who knows exactly what they're looking for, the best time to hunt it, and how to stay hidden from suspicion is successful because they do not have to look beyond themselves and the powers that guide them. To better focus when tracking—especially in colder areas—on-the-move meditations center the mind and clear away doubts.

Many hunters perform this exercise without even realizing it. It is such a part of the process that one carries it out instinctually as their energies build with the hope and anticipation for a successful expedition.

1. Carefully walk with slow and silent steps, placing each footfall with purpose.

2. Scan the area moving just the eyes from as far left to as far right as possible, slow and steady. Listen, absorb the entire scene. Let your sense take over.

3. If something draws your gaze to a specific area slowly look in that direction and turn the body. Control every limb, every breath.

Patience

There is much waiting when on a hunt. A person has to find comfort in the quiet. Instead of filling the head with background noise, a hunter must keep the ears ready and the sights set.

A hunter cannot properly seek out prey without a solid link to nature and themselves. Perfecting patience takes a lifetime. As age offers the benefits of greater understanding through education and experience so does each hunting trip.

Failure is one of the best learning tools—it immediately delivers the outcome. A person cannot move forward without overcoming those upsets. This leads them to learn from their mistakes and work to improve on them.

To work on practicing more patience deep though and/or meditations helps a hunter stay entertained with just their brain. Patience comes to those who think. The people who can make peace with their minds and relax their spirits know what it means to take their time and put care into each action.

1. Find a spot to blend in and wait.

2. Gaze beyond, scanning the scene. Compare it to previous experiences. Recall how it is similar to past explorations.

3. Then seek out the subtle differences. What makes this spot, this moment, different?

4. Think of how you are different. What is it you're here for? Are you just hungry for wild meat or does the fresh air and tree cover offer more?

5. Take in the image. Are there those you would share it with? Or is this a getaway, a place for you alone?

6. Let the thoughts wander in these realms while remaining alert to the surroundings.

Self-Reliance

Once confident in your weapon and the ability to properly use it, hunting is less about the equipment and more about self-reliance. The body becomes better trained to act with honor and react thoughtfully to their surroundings. Growing accustomed to small animals and feather fowl reminds humans that no matter how far we stray from our natural tendencies, the world is still waiting for us. It moves in its own time and hosts a slower, gentler aspect.

The mind focuses on details that stretch great spans. Instead of only seeing what is in front of the face, hunters survey the area. They tap into primal instincts and are more equipped to handle the unexpected.

Hunting has the potential to balance one's entire being. The energies come together. The universe and/or the god(s) are more present. The power it/they present can elevate.

Being self-reliant enough to fend for my own purpose and hunt for food while listening to my instincts hosts enough power to draw out new abilities.

Heightened senses lead to more animal encounters. More animal encounters lead to higher respects. Higher respects lead to stronger ties and decisions, which lead to fulfillment and prosperity.

To strengthen trust in self-reliance:

1. Stop during a hunt.

2. Kneel down.

3. Gaze up to the sky and close your eyes. Forget sight. Most animals rely on much more than what they see.

4. Feel the sky above and how it mingles with the habitat. Sniff the earthy scents coming from different directions. Place your hands on the ground and absorb the energies of the dirt and rock beneath.

5. Visualize returning to the earth you came from. Face the prospect of death as your kill will soon do.

6. Meditate on what must be done and how to carry it out.

7. Reconcile yourself with death, respecting it as a natural part of life. For humans to live others must die: whether a plant growing and thriving from the ground, a fish swimming in a brook, or a deer rushing through the trees. Make peace with that and balance this weight with admiration for the plants and animals who make way for others.

Respect

Hunting for meat to consume involves a person as completely as possible. They are present to witness the origins of energy transference and survival. To use the power of hunting instincts, one must look upon their prey with high regard.

No creature is ever without the need to seek out other beings. Whether for companionship, enjoyment, knowledge, or nourishment, life is reliant on life. Once this is accepted and acknowledged, hunters are more apt to help preserve lands and protect game. Learning to take only what is needed instead of becoming obsessed or fanatical comes with this balance.

When entering an ecosystem with the intent to hunt, honorable hunters pay their respects. This is an ongoing ritual that comes when gazing upon small creatures, after shooting an animals, and when leaving the space. It is done through subtle moments or even a slight gesture based on one's individual attitude and personal development, but for the most part it goes:

1. As you enter the land, stop and really see it for what it is. Think of the beauty and be grateful to share in it.

2. When spotting a rare bird or a small animal, stop and observe it. Smile at the creature and think of how your intended target must see you.

3. After a kill, before moving from shooting space and going to the carcass, look to the body. Breathe in the act, how just a moment sooner the animal stood alive and now it is down.

4. As you are leaving, just before you exit completely, turn back to the area and take a moment to look upon its pleasing view. Think of all you experienced (not just with the hunter's instinct) and feel gratitude.

Wasteless

To take a life and feed from its remains affects the spirit whether a person acknowledges the changes or not. It can lead toward further enlightenment or degradation. Honorable hunters elevate themselves in many ways. Beyond caring for nature and the creatures they seek, using as much of the body as possible and leaving the rest for scavengers is the main goal, as is picking up after one's self.

Humans have a tendency to take what they can. The instinct to collect resources is still strong, but the urge to keep surrounding areas clean is not as prominent as it once was. The idea is that more people equal more waste, but that does not have to be true if each person conserves their resources and makes use of them to the fullest extent.

It is still possible for people to minimize waste to only biodegradables. It takes much care and preparation but is easily done in the field when hunting.

Instead of bringing processed snacks, fresh fruits and vegetables or even a log of sausage is more beneficial to the body as well as the land. Reusable water bottles or canteens are easy to obtain and handy for use as they are more apt to handle extreme temperatures than disposable plastics. Apple cores, roots, or uneaten stalks can be cast into the woods for animal consumption or to break down.

Then comes the more complicated business of field dressing kills and cutting up parts. Field dressing is a standard practice. Gutting the fresh kill to prepare it for butchering is best done in the wild so any internal organs or parts which the hunter does not wish to use can be left for scavengers or buried to enrich the earth.

Despite the gruesome view society takes on this practice, like all aspects of hunting and fending for one's self, even the butchering of a creature can be respectful and spiritual. Once the kill is transported to a suitable butchering environment, blessing the meat as chunks are cut away fuses one's energies further into their food. Finding uses for horns, hide, hooves, and bones, such as instruments, handles, clothing, jewelry, and more, makes further justification for the loss of life.

These items can also be buried or burned in a ritual. For hunters who send their meat to a trusted processor, they should ask that the excess be returned for the rite, not disposed.

To honor the animal once its body has been processed and dispose of unusable items:

1. Gather the materials together and place on ground beside burial site or inside the bonfire brush before lighting.

2. Kneel before them and meditate on the animal that was killed, how it enriched the forest in its own life, and yours in death.

3. Stand and brush hands over the ground then raise them up to the sky. Chant, sing, or shout of how your lives are entwined. Circle the materials, dancing or walking slowly then picking up the pace. When your energies are at their peak, bury the items or light the fire.

4. Stand before the burial site or the fire and meditate on the powers that grow within. Bow to the scene. Thank the god(s)/universe and close the rite.

Fishing

To fish for one's food is meditation. Patience and skill are somewhat necessary, but it is a love of water and the shores that truly bonds a fisher to their purpose.

Instead of tracking down a kill, fishing is more about drawing prey to the line. One must find a good place to set up and wait. The setting depends on the type of fishing a person engages in. Fly-fishing is best done among rushing rapids. Cool waters flow freely revealing delights that abound below. Pole fishing is more calming. Slow, quiet lakes and ponds offer up catches. Boat fishing is the gateway between worlds. It can be successful in any body of water when steered by knowing hands.

Having the right equipment isn't about the cost of the rod. I don't spend much on my equipment. It's not necessary since I know how to tie hooks on properly, and enjoy digging up bait from my own backyard.

This less expensive endeavor allows self-reliance for any income level. It breeds higher respects for bodies of water and the creatures that inhabit them. Like hunting, fishing offers up a sacrifice and a bond to the land that increases power in those with honorable tactics. Fishing holds age-old wisdom that waits to be drawn from even shallow pools.

Patience

A truly patient fisher may not always find a catch but they always retrieve knowledge from the water and the land. Patience is mentioned all throughout life. Anyone can be good and kind when they do not have to wait, but when tried and tested by time or the need to persevere, they will display different qualities. Fishing is a constant exercise in patience.

Fly fishing is more active, but its catches are livelier. They do not come as easily and so the person carrying out the act has to keep a cool head and focus on how best to bring in the fish on the other end of the hook. In addition to controlling their body, they must also control the mind. A sort of trance wraps around them. The spell of finding what one seeks is enhanced with this action. For standard fishing, the act is more drastic. I love to stand and cast out to let my mind drift with the current. Contemplation is imminent. The sky and the grasses hint at answers to questions I didn't even know I held within. After a while, the pole moves or I feel a tug and I'm jerked into action battling against the fish.

So often in life we are forced into unsuspected moments of action. They present themselves in public when someone needs help or tensions build. Knowing how to discern the best way to approach the situation comes from practice like that found just sitting with a fishing pole.

To pull focus back to the intention when patience is waning, personal meditation serves the higher self.

1. Set down the object of your frustration. If injured, hold the cut or blister tight.

2. Close your eyes. Breathe deep. Shout, yell, or chant short words about the situation and how it will not deter you.

3. Bow your head and visualize yourself achieving your goal.

4. Open your eyes and continue fishing or save it until your next fishing excursion (if needed).

Respect

The magic of personal power increases when we are self-reliant. That is not to say that helping others or accepting help when in need is wrong. Those who are better able to care for themselves are in a position to aid others, and so it is a cycle that never ends. Above all, we should always strive to help ourselves before looking to others.

Hunting requires a lot of energy. Some elements of fishing do as well, but fishing does not require as much land to be covered. A person need not overexert themselves when fishing. Instead of stalking prey, they present their food to them.

Sitting still does not come easily for everyone; neither does remaining alert and prepared for action when sitting still. Balancing the act of readiness with the ability to control one's movements is a subtle art. When an individual masters complete control over their body, they are better able to interact within their environment.

Being mindful of the creatures one seeks and respecting them for their role in life delivers a different form of respect that forms when confident in the ability to rely on yourself. Honorable fishers rely on themselves to catch food but also reflect on the water and its meaning in life. They learn to slow down and soak up the air, the ground. This appreciation fosters a love that forms like a protection spell. It wraps around a person and eases their fears for the future.

One cannot fully respect themselves and their nature if they do not respect the world surrounding them. Fish are living, breathing beings that have the power to collectively shape an ecosystem and shift water quality. People may benefit from their fillets, but fish do more for humans than nourish their diets. They fertilize the banks and balance bug and small water creature populations.

They are a perfect example of beings that thrive in closed environments, a perfect example of positive outcomes in the wild. We are thus helped to look to the past before jumping ahead toward potentially damaging practices.

There is much respect owed to the creatures that directly provide more balance in our lives. Meditating on the area in which you are fishing and the creatures a person seeks is one direct method for gaining this ability. To do this one must:

1. Find a comfortable position.

2. Gaze upon the water. Scan the surface. See the mirrored images of the sky and surroundings. Look to the banks and study each space where the water meets the shore.

3. Place a hand on the ground and dig fingers in a bit if not too dry. Feel the grains, the clumps of earth beneath your grasp.

4. Stand and walk to the water. Crouch before it. Place the other hand in the water. Swirl it around. Watch the ripples dance away.

5. Think of the numerous creatures beneath the dirt and water. Now think of yourself and your reasons for coming. Is it just to catch fish, or is there more? Is it for a break? For the quiet or time to think without being interrupted?

6. Look to the sky and breathe deep. Be thankful for the ability to stop and take a breath. Then get to fishing.

Wasteless

Human waste has become an inescapable problem. The modern age has brought us forward so fast that the basics of balance and decency are still righting themselves. Thankfully, nothing is ever too far gone. Everyone can alter their behavior enough to create solutions instead of adding to the problem.

Food waste is one of the greatest tragedies of modern times. In certain areas of the globe, humans have such an abundance of resources that they are bursting at the seams, while half a world away people are starving to death.

Reducing consumption, taking only what is necessary, and using all the leftover parts of what one eats may not fill stomachs or enrich impoverished areas but it does save resources so they can be better shared and distributed. If the general population took more time to carefully choose what they put into their bodies and set aside a portion of nonperishables for those less fortunate, the impact would be earth shaking.

As individuals, fishers have a duty to take on this philosophy and conserve what they can. Once the fish is descaled and its body cleaned, the inedible parts make a perfect fertilizer to enrich the land.

When you compost or bury fish parts in a garden, flowers absorb the nutrients, and vegetables and fruits turn the waste into fuel for their purpose. The powers that connect everything return the animal's remains to the soil and reward the fisher for their efforts and care. The physical benefits can be witnessed within weeks, depending on the time of year. Seeing one's own actions make a positive impact aids thought processes, but also displays a fuller, more brilliant link to the god(s)/universe.

To honor the fish and your land once the body has been processed:

1. Gather the materials together in bowl and place it on the ground beside the burial site. Bring a container of water as well.

2. Kneel before the remains and meditate on the fish that was or were killed, how it or they enriched the waters in its own life, and now yours in death.

3. Raise a hand up to the sky. Chant, sing, or shout of how your lives are entwined. Stand and look to the bowl. Circle it, dancing or walking slow, then picking up the pace.

4. When your energies are at their peak, bury the items.

5. Take up the water and pour it over the site saying words to seal the spot and consecrate the ground.

6. Meditate on the powers that grow within. Bow to the scene. Thank the god(s)/universe and close the rite.

Foraging

Knowing where your food comes from is essential to ensuring it is pure for the body and the mind. Taking the extra step to find and pick your own food unlocks that knowledge. Creating a direct link to the planet and our energies that tie us to the land beyond time and understanding is important.

Foraging through blueberry patches or finding the ripest apples on a tree is a forgotten ritual. The strength one gains from the experience and joy of plucking their own food from the vine is immeasurable. Faces and energies are drawn forth through the greenery. Berries paint the mind with possibility. If one can forage for their own food, they begin to realize just how much more they can actually do. It breeds self-respect but also a higher regard for the very lands beneath one's feet.

This openhanded behavior spreads. It increases and encourages others. It also expands the powers within. The love and laughter that come with giving spills into all aspects of life and charges spellwork tenfold.

Respect

Finding the right place to forage is trickier than it was in generations past. Instead of simply scouring surrounding areas, private property is everywhere. For those who own a little piece of the earth (for as much as person can "own" something that exists with or without them) or have family or friends with property, this is an inviting practice. Traveling to a countryside or nice little area tucked away from the rest of the world takes us back to our origins. It softens the spirit but also better shapes ambitions as the forager focuses their eyes on the discovery of ripe foods ready for the taking.

For those who do not know anyone willing to share this experience, many local farms open their gates to the public. Unlike hunting and fishing, foraging is best done in groups, with loved ones who will also benefit from the activity. Done together, foraging strengthens not only our ties to nature and nutrition, but also allows us to experience the beauty of sharing a meal in the comfort of dear friends and family members.

With each trip, each season of searching and picking, a stronger sense of what is most important intensifies. The snacks and meals that come from the fruit of one's labors taste better. They host a special energy that boosts mental health and encourages spiritual growth.

Honoring nature and the gifts it provides is a higher respect. Instead of just consuming whatever is most convenient, those who forage and take part in the entire process become bonded to the planet in new ways.

A foraging adventure once a month or at least a season is enough to bring a person back to their senses. Growing a few herbs or vegetables rounds these experiences out, welcomes them into everyday life. Accepting more responsibility a little at a time keeps a person in control without overwhelming them.

Once you are practiced in foraging or if you are already an avid gardener and/or local farm supporter, the following meditation that can be carried out while picking food:

1. Walk up to the plants. Stop and close your eyes. Breathe in the freshness.

2. Visualize your ancestors standing with you. Think of how they would have seen this abundance and what these kinds of foods meant to them.

3. Open eyes and pluck the first piece of fruit or dig up the first vegetable. Hold it before your mouth for a moment, then bite into it, raw and unwashed, straight from the soil (best for organic foods grown without pesticides).

4. Smile at the plants still heavy with food. Bow to them and offer your thanks for the harvest.

5. Fill basket or sack with as much as needed keeping this gratitude in mind.

6. When finished, tap the ground with your food. Gaze up to the sky. Feel the power of the elements washing over everything and do not forget that it is a blessing.

Spells

Food holds the power to soothe and heal. Bringing home fresh ingredients obtained by my own prowess allows my energies to pour into the meals created with them. Working with foods obtained by one's own efforts is an unparalleled event.

A kitchen becomes a home to those who put their energy into it. It houses many energies, meditations, and spells for those who tap into their spiritual self. The following spells are just a few of the possibilities directly linked to meats and/or fruits and vegetables brought to the table through hunting, fishing, or foraging.

TO BLESS A BOAT

MATERIALS NEEDED: Self, boat, sage, bottle of wine

TO PREPARE: Open the bottle of wine and meditate on it. Slide a finger into the bottle and pour your energies in the liquid to bless it. Only bless a boat once it is waterborne. Do *not* perform this rite on land.

THE WORK:

1. Bring materials to the boat. Stand at the stem/bow (front) and light the sage (this can be done at the dock outside of the boat or inside before pushing off). Place hand upon the stem/bow and chant or sing for sturdy travels and good fishing.

2. Walk down to the stern (back) of the boat and do the same, letting the sage burn along the way.

3. Now walk back to the front and drink a swig of wine from the bottle. Feel the rush surge through your body like the water against the boat. Chant or sing of bonding your ship to your purpose.

4. Walk to the stern and pour the rest of the wine over the back end. Bow to the sacrifice and ground yourself to the vessel.

WEAPONRY BLESSING

A hunter's tool is their weapon. How it is used determines the hunter's rate of success, something true for anyone who wishes to kill their own food and deeply understand the powers of nature and the energies that bind us to our actions.

Bonding with my weapon better served me and those around me because I cherish the values of safety and self-reliance. Safety prevents accidents caused by ignorance or unconventional use. When charmed or blessed by its keeper, a weapon becomes enhanced. This rite seals the fate of both the person and the weapon they possess. It melds the intentions, locking the possibilities in place.

To bless a weapon:

MATERIALS NEEDED: Self, weapon, purpose candle and candle(s) to represent the god(s)/universe, handful of dirt on plate, bowl of blessed salt, bowl of blessed water, sage, and matches

TO PREPARE: Set an altar or table with the deity candles at the head, facing north. Place the purpose candle in the center between the deity candles if there are more than one. Set the salt and water bowls at either side east and west and put the weapon closest to you at the south end horizontal to the candles. The plate of dirt can be set before the weapon or on the ground in front of the altar and the weapon where you will perform the act.

THE WORK:

1. Cast a circle by walking around the altar/table with the salt and sprinkling it as you speak words of sealing the circle in the name of the god(s)/universe by the power of earth, air, fire, and water. Then repeat in the opposite direction with the water.

2. Cleanse the space with burning sage.

3. Now stand before your weapon facing the purpose candle. Take up the handful of dirt and sprinkle it down to the plate with both hands, whispering, chanting, or singing of balance and the understanding that weapons are sacred tools.

4. Light the god(s)/universe candle(s) asking for the greater purpose to bless this ritual.

5. Kneel before the weapon and hold hands just above it. Close your eyes and meditate. Visualize yourself hunting with honor.

6. Open eyes and light the purpose candle. Meditate on its flame. Feel its warmth and build your energies.

7. Take up your weapon and hold it over the candle (stand if necessary). Chant, sing, or whisper to mix your energies with the weapon to let it serve you, protect you, and aid in keeping good health.

8. Put the weapon back on the altar and bow. Clear the mind and meditate on the weapon.

9. When exhausted, lie down and ground yourself.

EQUIPMENT BLESSING

Hunters bless their weapons, and honorable fishers may bless their poles, their boots, and even their boats to seal the power between themselves and their purpose. The rite for blessing poles and boots is similar to blessing a weapon.

To bless a fishing pole:

Materials Needed: Self, weapon, purpose candle and candle(s) to represent the god(s)/universe, fishing knife, bowl of blessed salt, bowl of muddy water, sage, and matches

To Prepare: Set an altar or table with the god(s) candles at the head, facing north. Place the purpose candle in the center between the deity candles if there are more than one. Set the salt and water bowls at either side, east and west. Put the fishing knife between you and the purpose candle horizontal to it. Then set the pole or boots closest to you at the south end horizontal to the candles.

The Work:

1. Cast a circle by walking around the altar/table with the salt and sprinkling it as you speak words of sealing the circle in the name of the god(s)/universe by the power of earth, air, fire, and water.

2. Cleanse the space with burning sage, walking a circle in the opposite direction.

3. Now stand before your pole/boots facing the purpose candle. Raise the pole or boots over the muddied water. With your dominant hand, cup a handful of muddy water and spill it over the pole or boots while whispering, chanting, or singing about balance and the understanding that these items are sacred tools.

4. Light the god(s)/universe candle(s) asking for the greater purpose to bless this ritual.

5. Kneel before the pole or boots and rub hands together above. Close your eyes and meditate. Visualize yourself fishing with honor.

6. Open eyes and light the purpose candle. Meditate on its flame. Feel its warmth and build your energies.

7. Take up your pole or the boots and hold over the candle (stand if necessary). Chant, sing, or whisper to mix your energies with the item(s), to let it serve you, protect you, and aid in keeping good health.

8. Put the pole or boots on the altar again and bow. Clear the mind and meditate on it/them.

9. When exhausted, lie down and ground yourself.

BLESSING A KILL

To respect what you eat is to respect yourself. To bless the food that came from another life is to bless your existence.

After a hunter brings down an animal, they have an opportunity to increase the energy that comes from the act of taking a life and bless that which now rests to bring it peace. Respect for nature and even prey does not require a blessing, but it does bring the entire experience together in one great rite.

The body is satisfied by the physicality of tracking and hunting. The mind is equipped when patient and self-reliant. The higher self charges under the surge of energy that comes when hitting the target but the act remains mundane.

Performing rites to bless the kill as well as a rite to bless your successful hunt takes very little time but affects a person greatly. To bless the kill:

MATERIALS NEEDED: Self, carcass

TO PREPARE: Hunt and kill an animal. Approach its body once the life has left with the last breath. Do this after blessing the kill if you carry out that rite as well.

THE WORK:

1. Stand before the creature.

2. Grab weapon and hold it over the animal horizontally. Look up to the sky. Whisper, chant, or sing of your connection to your weapon, your life, and to the hunt.

3. Look down and close your eyes. Clear your mind and let the energy inside grow. Feel it increase with those around you.

4. Bow to the body. Field clean and find use for as much of the remains as humanely possible. That is a grounding rite in itself.

BLESSING THE FISH

Once pulled from the water, a fish struggles. Its will to live is strong and so it is important to end the suffering quickly. Suffocation is a terrifying process. For fishers who are equipped, cutting through the forehead and stabbing the brain of the dying creature with a fishing knife puts a quick end to misery.

Taking a life this way puts the action in perspective—we are not just plucking an animal from the water and eating it, we are ending a life.

In honor of yourself, your actions, and the fish, a simple blessing may be performed.

FISHER'S BLESSING

MATERIALS NEEDED: Self, catch

TO PREPARE: Catch a fish and end its suffering quickly. Then hold it in your hands.

THE WORK:

1. For smaller fish, balance it in one palm and hold the other hand over its body. For larger fish, lay the body on the ground and kneel before it and rub the scales with both hands.

2. Look up to the sky. Whisper, chant, or sing of your connection to this creature, your life, and the water.

3. Look at the fish and close your eyes. Clear your mind and let the energy inside you grow. Feel it increase with that of your surroundings.

4. Bow to the body. Put it on ice until you are ready to bring it home and clean it. Find as much use for the remains as humanely possible. That is a grounding rite in itself.

PLANT-BASED DISH BLESSING

MATERIALS NEEDED: Self, ingredients, cooking pan or pot

TO PREPARE: Wash the food and cut, peel, or ready for cooking.

THE WORK:

1. Stand before the dish just before it is cooked.

2. Place your fingertips just resting lightly on the dish. Close your eyes and clear your mind.

3. Focus your energies on how they expanded when you were foraging. Now take that freedom and let it increase your personal power. Visualize the spark inside growing until it flows into the food.

4. Chant, sing, or whisper words of blessing the food as it has blessed you already.

5. Open your eyes, bow to the dish, and cook. Do this with each dish if serving multiples.

PLANT-BASED MEAL BLESSING

MATERIALS NEEDED: Self, already cooked/prepared dishes, taper candles in holders (at least two but as many as you would like), matches, wine or water

TO PREPARE: Clean, prep, and cook food however you like. Set on table when ready. Fill glass(es) with water or wine.

THE WORK:

1. Stand at the head of the table and bow to the foods and anyone else partaking of the meal.

2. Raise arms up and chant, sing, or whisper words of thanks and gratitude for the meal (and the opportunity to share it if you are not alone).

3. Light each candle, welcoming the elements and the god(s)/universe.

4. Take up the water or wine and toast to good health and good fortune. Then enjoy the comforts of your work.

HEALING FOOD SPELL

MATERIALS NEEDED: Ingredients and self

TO PREPARE: Clean ingredients.

THE WORK:

1. Before prepping the food, touch your fingertips to it and close your eyes.

2. Visualize the healing energies within you like a ball of colored light.

3. Let it grow and expand through your limbs and out your fingers into the raw ingredients.

4. Now prep the food. As you peel, cut, season, or mix, focus on pushing out all of your healing powers into the dish.

5. When ready, cook it. Bow once you are finished.

6. Eat or share with someone in need.

CALMING FOOD SPELL

MATERIALS NEEDED: Ingredients, self, matches, and single candle

To PREPARE: Clean ingredients.

THE WORK:

1. Before prepping, breathe deep and think of the foods' origins.

2. Visualize how they slowly sprout and grow to form into a healthy, nutritious offering.

3. Meditate on your origins. Recall how you sprouted through life and have grown. What have you offered to the world in return for this opportunity to exist?

4. Now prep the food. As you peel, cut, season, or mix focus on all your accomplishments and good deeds. Let those memories soak into your thoughts.

5. When ready, cook the food and stand before it, simmering in your own purpose. Light the candle and chant, sing, or whisper words of relaxing after hard work and effort.

6. Sit before the candle and focus on the flame, clearing the mind and resting.

7. Once ready, set the table around the candle and eat or share the dish or meal with someone who could use it.

INCREASED ENERGIES FOOD SPELL

MATERIALS NEEDED: ingredients, self, two to three candles to represent the god(s)/universe and yourself, water or wine

To PREPARE: Clean ingredients.

THE WORK:

1. Meditate on your actions as you prepare food.

2. Let the energy of crafting a meal from scratch build. Pour that power into the food with each movement. Visualize it glowing within you and sliding out from your fingertips.

3. Place the dish(es) on the table before cooking/finishing in front of the candles. Place the god(s)/universe candle(s) at the head and the "self" candle between the deity candle(s) and the dishes in front of you.

4. Raise your arms over the food and close your eyes. Chant, sing, or whisper words thanking the gods and promise to look for signs of their presence and to listen to their guidance more closely.

5. Cook or finish dish(es) and meditate on the candles while waiting. Feel the warmth from the candle flames and your own life source combine and flow within you. Let it grow and take over.

6. When the meal is ready, set the table around the candles and bless the food with words of gratitude. Acknowledge the power of feeding the body and the soul. This is best done as a solitary practice but a close friend or family member can be invited to share the meal.

9
HANDIWORK

There is a freedom in handiwork. The sense of accomplishment that comes with creating a machine or finishing glasswork reaches into our creation instinct.

No matter how we are created, creation makes us feel alive. Focusing the body and the mind on a specific endeavor that rewards hard work and diligence touches the spirit. When I craft something, it better links myself and others to my unique talents and reveals a greater purpose.

Connecting to the future by carrying on certain elements of the past balances my being. I pride myself on being able to craft my own items; it drives an understanding and appreciation for my role in existence, and it inspires me to create spells that protect and guide the energies surrounding everyone.

Woodworking

One of the oldest, most instinctual crafts is woodworking. When truly balanced, the act of carving a block connects a person's needs to their desires and allows them to intertwine the two in a perfect display of harmony and self-expression. Those who craft with wood have an obligation to respect and preserve the materials they use. Conserving wood for specific projects is helpful, as is supporting the planting of more trees both locally and globally. Together, both actions ensure the future of the craft without destroying its essential element.

Beyond this, certain instinctual energies rise to the surface. It breeds power and creates the best atmosphere for spellwork. Spells ingrained in the fibers have the ability to last beyond specific timelines.

Visions of grandparents or other ancestors who have passed on come to mind more easily. There is a reason the elderly are so insistent on teaching the young—they know what it means to see traditions bond people across generations and that a new skill offers new possibilities.

Woodworking recalls elders' wisdom. When focused properly, a person falls under its trance. This state can be nudged into guided meditations which offer perspective. (This is only true for hand tool woodworking; saws require more conscious control.)

Our actions hold more weight when we truly learn the meaning of love and respect for family and what it means to both look up to those who came before us and smile on those who will eventually supersede us. Carving a toy or decoration becomes symbolic of that shared knowledge and the energies we wish to impart to others. Try this on your own:

1. Meditating on the wood creates a balanced connection. Work on the wood, carving or shaping as intended.

2. As your body relaxes into the motion, also relax your eyes. Gaze upon the work but let your mind drift as you go.

3. Think of the wood, where it came from, what kind of tree it once was. See it as it once lived.

4. Now focus on the wood's new purpose. The tree has already fallen, but it lives on in your hands. What you create will carry its spirit and share it with anyone who sees it.

5. Feel the wood's energy. How does it speak to you? What will it do for you or others in the future?

6. Listen and absorb the power of mingling your purpose with that of a fallen tree.

Spells

Woodworking spells are crafted in much the same way as the object itself. It takes patience and focus to get the intended outcome. They should only be attempted after a person is used to the act and has successfully explored woodworking meditation.

STICK CARVING SIGIL

Materials Needed: Stick, carving knife, self

To Prepare: Focus on the need or purpose. Think of a simple term or phrase to represent it. Now reduce the duplicate letters and arrange them into a single image.

The Work:

1. Take a walk outside and find a stick suitable for carving.

2. Sit and meditate on it. Let the fresh air tickle the senses and expand your energies. Visualize your power as a light and pour it into the stick.

3. Now focus on your need or purpose. Whisper, sing, or chant this and carve the sigil along the wood as many times as possible.

4. Bow to the stick and place it somewhere safe. Keep it for a full moon cycle, then burn in a full moon fire, releasing the energies outward to continue on. Depending on the spell's subject, it can take shape during the month or may not come to be until after the stick burns, but patience and focus are necessary.

WOOD BLOCK CHARM

Materials Needed: Uncarved wood block, carving tools, self

To Prepare: Bless the wood by meditating on it and the tree it came from.

The Work:

1. Take up the block and think of the person (or yourself if keeping) you wish it to protect.

2. Focus on that purpose and begin to carve the block into the object you wish to create.

3. Build your energies and feel them charged within you. Now push that energy into the wood.

4. While you do so chant, sing, or whisper words to seal this fate. Repeat the phrase throughout the entirety of the carving. It will be tiresome, but it is important to keep repeating the words. Take breaks as needed, but try to finish the project in a single day for the best outcome.

5. When finished, kiss the final product and visualize it watching over the intended owner.

6. Gift to a loved one, or place where it will be seen (if it is for yourself).

FURNITURE SPELL/BLESSING

MATERIALS NEEDED: Finished furniture carved by your own hand, blessed salt and water, candle and matches, sage

TO PREPARE: Bless the salt and the water by individually sitting before them and touching with fingertips, pouring your energies into the elements. Place the candle on top of the furniture and the other materials before it.

THE WORK:

1. Stand before the furniture.

2. Light the sage and walk around it in a circle. Whisper, chant, or sing about cleansing the new creation. Wave the sage above it, then extinguish and set aside.

3. Take up the salt and toss a small bit onto the surface of the wood.

4. Dip your fingertips into the water and sprinkle over the salt on the wood.

5. Reach up and sing, chant, or whisper about the wood's new purpose. Ask the god(s)/universe to bless its new form.

6. Now light the candle. Walk or dance around the furniture letting the warmth of the candle fuel your sense of accomplishment. Be glad to see your work supporting an element that could destroy it. See your creation as more than just an object but also a manifestation of your efforts.

7. When your energies reach their peak, turn to the furniture and hold your arms over it. Send that power into your work.

8. When finished, ground yourself. Eat and/or drink to your success.

Mechanics

Building a machine takes more than just grit and muscle. It is not the work of a storybook wizard or fairy. Mechanical understanding is a tangible skill, and yet there are still ties to the higher self, a greater sense of purpose, and even instinctual magic.

The strength required to put together a car, or even the skill one's hands must possess to piece together a smaller technology, does not rest in physical power alone. Strength of mind and the intelligence needed to build new contraptions has been many populations' greatest asset, and yet without some outside purpose, some greater goal, the meaning crumbles.

For the people who appreciate mechanics *and* its ability to draw out new energies not often viewed as connected with magic or spirituality, there is wisdom waiting in each component. It means stepping away from letting others do the work to understand all of a machine's connections and parts.

When approaching a new project, educating yourself on basic concepts or finding a good teacher/mentor brings wisdom forth. Learning from an aged mechanic or teaching yourself to pass on those lessons learned through trial and error links you as a human to creation's possibilities and opens up your capacity for higher thought, allowing you to ponder your place in everything. This reflection brings a form of balance that goes beyond survival—it makes life an art.

Mechanics are not generally known for outwardly expressing themselves. So much of their craft is solitary or requires concentration, but it is the meditative work that aids them to finish their projects and help others. Not everyone has the ability to throw themselves into labor of this kind, but for those who do it and do so with a deeper bond to their instincts and the god(s)/universe, what they craft is a spell in itself.

To bring the elements and instincts out when exercising mechanical skills, a person must find meditation and ritual in the work.

1. Begin work on the project.
2. Clear the mind and let the actions build energy.
3. Follow the repetitious work into a trance. The mind will focus itself and images, words, or thoughts will come. Explore them one at a time.
4. Gain some control over the journey through the brain while your hands continue working. Seek out the greater purpose. What does all of this mean to you, your loved ones, and others?

5. As the answers come or more ideas appear, remain fixed on the task but pull back to reality and the present. Finish the work and celebrate your efforts.

Spells

Humans put their energies into the things they create whether they know it or not, which is why some handmade objects host a light or electricity that cannot be otherwise explained. Directing that energy for a specific purpose leads to wonderful possibilities, but the basic ideals lay in simple spells that produce strong outcomes.

The effort put forth determines how much of an impact one can make with their actions, thoughts, and will. When combined with care and duty, spells performed in mechanics are just as useful as the machines that humans take for granted.

FINDING PURPOSE/GUIDANCE SPELL

MATERIALS NEEDED: Parts, tools, self, wine or water

TO PREPARE: Make sure you have all the materials needed to build the machine

THE WORK:

1. Place wine or water off to a spot close to your work space but far enough away to remain untouched.

2. Begin building the machine.

3. Focus your hands on doing the work and relax the mind.

4. As you put each piece together, whisper, chant, or think/envision in search of purpose or guidance through the endeavor and what comes after: life.

5. Repeat these words all throughout the entire creation. When reaching appropriate benchmarks take breaks, but then refocus as soon as starting again.

6. As the machine grows near to finishing certain answers, ideas should form. Explore them. Let them carry your thoughts where they need to be.

7. When finished, stand before the machine. Raise your arms and walk or dance in a circle around it. Walk to the wine or water and raise to your

lips, pausing to be thankful for the accomplishment and toast yourself and the powers that led you to meet this goal. Then drink long and hard.

8. Splash a small portion on or in front of the machine. Chant, sing, or speak of the god(s)/universe and your gratitude as you pursue further guidance and meaning. Bow to the endeavor and blessed be.

MACHINE PROTECTION SPELL

MATERIALS NEEDED: Finished machine, self, sage, candle and matches

TO PREPARE: Finish the mechanics and gather materials. Place candle on the centermost portion of the machine.

THE WORK:

1. Stand at the front of the machine. Light the sage. Wave it over the machine from front to back and then top to bottom.

2. Hold arms up to the sky and whisper, chant, or sing about cleansing the machine.

3. Now light the candle. Place hands on either side of the candle and stare at the flame. Feel the heat rising inside you.

4. Close your eyes. Let the energy build and grow until it slips out through your hands. Visualize it charging the machine.

5. Chant, sing, or whisper its new purpose of protection.

6. Open eyes and dance or walk around the car, circling slowly at first, then pick up the pace and go faster and faster until exhausted. Place hands on the machine once more and seal the rite with saliva or blood. Kiss or spit on it. (A small cut will offer enough blood to finish the ritual but is not necessary.)

7. Rest and ground yourself.

SOLITARY SATISFACTION SPELL

MATERIALS NEEDED: Finished machine, self, cloth

TO PREPARE: Finish the machine

THE WORK:

1. Close your eyes. Meditate on the cloth, pouring your energies into it. Visualize all the hard work you put into your machine and let that power slip through you and charge the cloth.

2. Stand before the machine. Hold the cloth in your dominant hand.

3. Breathe deep. Clear mind. Focus energies on the machine and how you are bonded to it after building it.

4. Go to the machine and wipe it down with the cloth. While doing so, sing, chant, or think words or images of pride in solitary endeavors.

5. Feel the instinctual pleasure of taking time away from everyone else to create something. Revel in it. Be proud of your accomplishment.

6. When done wiping down every inch of the machine, stand before it and gaze on your creation with pride. Let this lone moment fill you with strength.

7. Bow to it and ready yourself to share this work with others.

Knitting/Crocheting

Yarn working is full of soft, warm energies. It is a useful tradition that allows parents to gift their children clothing, blankets, and other items infused with their energies. As gifts for friends and other family members, fabric arts offer us the opportunity to personalize a gift or share a special skill that has survived well into the modern age and secure hopes that these traditions will be carried on well into the future.

A special form of magic lives in yarn work. It is a gentler form, but one that lightens curses, soothes anxiety, and lifts the weight of fear. Like all handiwork, knitting and crocheting provide a person time to balance themselves. Yarn itself symbolizes simple solutions to complex problems because no matter how knotted a ball of yarn may become, it can be straightened out and used for a greater purpose.

Gifting hand knitted toys or clothing keeps my instinct to help others alive. It reminds me that no matter how many machines and factories produce goods, people always have the ability to take raw materials and turn them into beautiful things. I love knowing how important my single pair of hands is. When I crochet, I invoke that power and transform it for loved ones.

Knitting and crocheting are truly crafts to be shared. When sitting and working, my brain explores all aspects of life. Even on the rare occasion that I make something for myself, the question of stitching a piece of warm clothing for someone less fortunate comes to mind.

The revelations derived from meditating while knitting or crocheting give the act new meaning. Instead of just working with yarn, the goal becomes a gift, the endeavor a journey. Purpose and value are instilled in the self when yarn working.

Guiding these thoughts with conscious meditation encourages this balance further:

1. Start working the rounds. Relax the mind.

2. Focus on the movements. Study each loop. Think of how a chain or round would not be possible without each individual stitch.

3. Imagine yourself as a stitch. Whether you wish to be or not you are linked to others, to family, friends, a community, and the world.

4. Question that role. Have you been a strong asset to yourself and others? Have you helped hold others up and have they kept you strong when your own abilities failed you? Are you part of a strong chain, surrounded by influences who give you the support you need to help others? How can you hold yourself higher to lift others up more?

5. Ponder the questions slowly throughout the yarn work. Let the answers lead you through possibilities for the future. Also follow memories where they may reveal new understandings.

6. When you reach a stopping point or have finished, hold the work in your lap and rub your fingers over the stitches. Let its meaning ease you. Even a weak stitch can be strong when supported properly.

Spells

When casting spells for the purpose of yarn working, there are two main aspects that come to light. A person can weave the energies while crafting the object, or they can charm the object post stitching. Both methods hold much power, but when infusing energies while working, the person must remain focused on the work. It is more potent, as each stitch calls upon the god(s)/universe for aid. It is like a mass of numerous prayers or a gathering of well-wishes to bring about the needed outcome.

Exercising these abilities through balance, meditation, and purpose leads to proper spellwork. Casting needs present themselves when a situation calls for it instead of whenever the mood to practice strikes. In this way, a sense of purpose leads specifically toward what I need rather than fleeting wants. I have grown used to this and learned to remain perceptive to the universe and trust in the urges that arise when I want to infuse my creations with helpful spells and share the gift of intuition with others.

CURSE-BREAKING YARN WORK

MATERIALS NEEDED: Yarn, knitting or crochet needle(s), self

TO PREPARE: Gather items and be prepared to sit.

THE WORK:

1. Begin crocheting or knitting a clothing item, such as a hat, gloves, or socks, for the person under the power of a curse.

2. Focus your energies. Let them build and grow as you create your first row or chain.

3. Chant, whisper, or sing of ending the negative situation.

4. Repeat these words while looping each stitch.

5. When finished hug the garment and then gift to the person under the curse.

HEALING POWER BLANKET

MATERIALS NEEDED: Yarn, knitting or crochet needle(s), oil diffuser, eucalyptus oil, sage, matches, and self

TO PREPARE: Place the oil diffuser near the work space and set the oil to warm. Gather items and dedicate time and focus to the endeavor.

THE WORK:

1. Sit with the yarn and materials in lap. Place one hand over the yarn and hold the needle(s) in the other hand. Close your eyes.

2. Visualize your life source glowing from within. Imagine that light growing through your body and slipping into the materials through your fingers until they hold an electricity of their own.

3. Begin crocheting or knitting the blanket. Make it a large one even if for a baby or young person. Breathe in the healing oil. Feel it reviving your body and continuously pour that energy into the blanket.

4. Envision the blanket as a medicine. Fill it with energies that soothe and mend, that smother out disease and ailments. Keep these images in mind throughout the entire construction.

5. When finished, stand and place the blanket on your seat. Light the sage and slowly wave it over one side, chanting, singing, or whispering a blessing of good health and healing powers. Flip the blanket and do the same for the other side.

6. Snuff out the sage and oil diffuser. Kiss the blanket and then use it for yourself or give it to someone in need.

COZY PROTECTION CHARM

MATERIALS NEEDED: Finished yarn work item, blessed salt and water, candle, matches, and any scraps of yarn cut while making the item

TO PREPARE: Knit or crochet item and finish the work. Keep any frayed ends or clipped yarn that was part of the creation. Set the altar with the candle at the head (preferably facing north). Place the salt east and the water west. Then sprinkle the frayed yarn bits around the finished product.

THE WORK:

1. After finishing a yarn work project, take the item and set it in the center of a table or altar.

2. Take up the salt and sprinkle a circle around the yarn work. Chant, sing, or whisper a blessing of protection. Toss a handful of salt on the item.

3. Take up the water and flick a circle around the yarn work while chanting, singing, or whispering a blessing of sealing the protection.

4. Light the candle and ask the god(s)/universe for the energy to offer protection.

5. Get up and walk or dance around the table going faster and faster to build up more power. When you feel your power has reached its peak, kneel in front of the item, place both hands on it, and close your eyes. Push your energies into the item while visualizing it glowing with protective energies. If you made the item to give to a specific person, envision them being protected by the power that now lives in the handmade item.

6. When finished, pick it up and carefully hold over the candle. Seal the rite with a kiss and a blessing of protection.

HOPEFUL YARN WORK

MATERIALS NEEDED: Finished yarn item and self

TO PREPARE: Finish the craft.

THE WORK:

1. Sit or kneel with the new object before you.

2. Close your eyes and clear the mind. Recall to mind the energy of being a child. How you hoped and dreamed for things that may or may not have happened. Great power lies in hope. Let it build.

3. Reach forward and hold object in both hands.

4. Meditate on a short-term goal. How has it eluded you? How have you come close to reaching it?

5. Now visualize the reasons to keep trying. Dig deeper. Feel the connection between accomplishment and purpose. How does this specific goal meet that end? Push the energy drawn forward into your new creation.

6. Now meditate on your biggest long-term goal. Why does it matter? What does it mean in the grand scheme of your life?

7. Envision yourself attaining it. Will it bring happiness, a thirst for more, or a balance in between? Reach out into the universe with your mind. Follow your instincts through your mind until you meet the core of your

soul. Are your hopes meaningful and if so, is it the gains or the acts that lead there that matter most?

8. Push all the remaining power and energy within your body out through your hands into the object.

9. Lie down and rest. Ground yourself to the earth once more.

10. Wear or use object as needed, or if more decorative hang or place in home where it will be seen and appreciated on a daily basis. Let it serve as a reminder of your hopes and the ability to meet them.

Sewing/Quilting

Like yarn work, sewing and quilting fabrics together has an essential role in human history. Primitive patching evolved into elaborate costumes and everything in between. Not everyone is a seamstress, but knowing how to sew a button onto a shirt or patch up torn pants and skirts is a skill that people still find useful today, as it saves resources and combats frivolity.

Tuning my instincts to sew clothing, other necessities, decorations, and toys pushes me to go beyond the mundane business of just meeting my needs; it fulfills other aspects of life, draws more potential while balancing new energies with calm steadiness. Threading a deeper link between myself and the clothing I wear is almost as important as trusting a doctor's hands when a wound needs to be stitched up.

For centuries, sewing and quilt work were one of life's central aspects. Now that the necessity is gone, it has been downgraded to a craft or a hobby, but those who are willing to test it out or are already versed in stitching will find the satisfaction of finishing an edge or hemming clothes isn't just about making something for fun. There is a deeper tie to the instinctual nature of providing for ourselves and others.

There is a different energy, a unique power that flickers inside this specific work. It opens the mind to look back while moving forward. Instead of going about daily life and just doing what everyone else is doing, quilting and sewing present a heightened existence.

Nurturing this higher sense and following it to further enlightenment comes through meditation. To do so (this is also helpful if having to give a person stitches):

1. Sit ready to work. Clear the mind. Breathe deep and take a moment to just sit still.

2. Begin stitching. With prick of the needle and pull of the thread focus your energies on steadying the mind. A steady mind creates a calm body.

3. Think of the pieces you are sewing together as a linear path toward completion. Visualize completing the work, but also see those who came before you as they are already finished with everything.

4. Envision how this work will be completed and what it means to you and others. Will it heal? Will it offer comfort? Will it inspire happiness?

5. Now look to the future while remaining conscious of each stitch. Your actions are keeping this ancient practice alive. Why does that matter? What does it mean to you and those who come after?

6. Finish the work and tie it off. Take a moment to examine your efforts and appreciate the final product.

Spells

All energies are connected. When using our own hands to create something useful as well as truly beautiful, the object absorbs and emits the power put into it. Not everyone can identify this power, but most will at least feel it in their own way.

For those who wish to be more conscious and meet their purpose without question, harnessing and dispersing this energy is powerful. Sewn items and quilts are perfect for spellwork because they can contain our energy. All hand-iwork may be worked into spells, but working with intention holds a stronger, more lasting aura that carries on a practitioner's wishes with or without renewal.

INCREASING ENERGY SPELL

MATERIALS NEEDED: Material, sewing items (machine or needle and thread, etc.), self

TO PREPARE: Plan your pattern/pin as needed.

THE WORK:

1. Before working, meditate on the needle. Focus your mind on utilizing the power it generates when in motion. Instead of building energies and pushing them outward, you will be drawing in the electricity generated by the needle as you use it.

2. Start sewing or quilting. Feed off of the heat building up around your hands. Every motion and action expresses energy. Feel the energy coming off of the motion, the needle like a little burst of light.

3. Draw that heat into the fabric and your body as you work. Continuously spread the energy from the motion out over the materials and through your body. Let it reach your brain and flow beyond.

4. When the item is finished, set it before you and stand. Raise your arms and chant, sing, or whisper of its power and what came from the item's creation.

5. Bend down and brush fingertips over the fabric. Then use or gift the item.

OVERCOMING OBSTACLES

MATERIALS NEEDED: Material, sewing items (machine or needle and thread, etc.), self

TO PREPARE: Plan your pattern/pin as needed.

THE WORK:

1. Sit ready to work on the materials. Meditate on the loose fabric. Rub your hands over them. Feel their potential to make something or to be discarded.

2. Begin sewing or quilting. Feel the heat building in and around your hands.

3. Now visualize the obstacle(s) before you, seeing them as if they were fraying the edges of the fabric. With each stitch, sew those obstacles into something new, something productive and useful.

4. Repeat this until finished. When you have finished, rub your hands over the work. Draw in the power of change and betterment. Feel how obstacles are not necessarily meant to be destroyed but sewn into a different pattern for your benefit.

5. Stand before the new item. Walk around it chanting, singing, or whispering of overcoming obstacles through new stitches, new methods for placing the fabrics or foundations of your interactions and issues with the problem.

6. Let your energies build as you move around. Go faster and faster. At the fastest point, stop and hold arms over the fabric. Pour this new energy into it.

7. See the end of the frays and lack of resolve.

8. Bow to your finished work and ground yourself.

TAPPING INTO ANCESTRAL POWER

MATERIALS NEEDED: Sewing materials and items (machine or needle and thread, etc.), a feather, candle, and self

TO PREPARE: Plan your pattern/pin as needed.

THE WORK:

1. Gather materials and begin the work. Meditate on the action of your hands, how they move over the material and keep everything together.

2. Visualize your mother's hands working, then your grandmother's, all wrinkled and veiny. Let the mind continue reaching back. Visualize the hands that came before your grandmothers and the hands before hers. See thimbles and unpolished nails; worn fingers, tired and blistered.

3. Keep exploring the hands that worked before yours until you reach a stopping point or finish the work.

4. Fold up your work and set it before you on the floor. Set the candle at your left and the feather to your right.

5. Spit in palm of hands and rub together.

6. Hold the candle over the fabric and light the wick. Chant, sing, or whisper request to connect with your ancestors. Call them to you by the power of earth, air, fire, and water in the name of the god(s)/universe.

7. Place the candle aside and grasp the feather. Rub it over the fabric from seam to seam. Relax your eyes as you watch the feather move. Now close your eyes, but keep brushing the feather over the material.

8. Images, voices, or sensations may grace you with knowledge from your heritage. Listen and absorb what is presented. Meditate on it.

9. When exhausted, lie down and balance your energies.

Glasswork

Glass and ceramics are known for exuding a classic energy. Blown from sand and shaped through various techniques, glasswork holds more spiritual potential than chemical.

Glassworking may be a rarity in this day in age, but even my own sister has dabbled in it and I have found that it serves as a reminder of forgotten philosophies, namely that humanity is not as breakable as it seems but does not always need specific instructions to thrive in strength and wisdom.

Like all handiwork, glassworking requires knowledge and training from an experienced glassblower, but this is just the foundation of the practice. How one shapes and blows the glass is defined by their energies and their creativity as a glassblower. For those who are perceptive, the materials and designing grow power. It is easy to discover magic and purpose when fulfilling wishes and promises.

Taking simple grains and melting sand into art or useful items strengthens the bond. It gives more opportunity for tapping into personal energies and melding them with the materials and how they will be used.

Pressing fingertips to a freshly dried stained-glass creation or holding a jar or pitcher one crafted themselves calls to the instinct that tells a person, "You are made to live a meaningful life. You are made for more."

Spells

Glassblowing spells capture energies, they hold them in the bubbles, and preserve them for the entirety of existence. This is why glass stained windows in churches are so moving. Even non-Christians can appreciate the colorations, the devoted energies put forth. It is akin to the architectural beauty of religious buildings in the Middles East, or the temples in India.

To better display or connect to that quieter, hidden side of spirituality, glassworks hold the power for Pagans or any spiritualist to craft and display that beautiful energy without associating it to buildings or closed doors. Spells to gift these finished objects certain energies and purpose are highly powerful and are meant for sacred ends.

SANCTITY BLESSING

MATERIALS NEEDED: Glass oven/annealing oven, sand/glass, glass pipe, heat resistant gloves, pipe stand, steel tweezers, wood block, grinding block, self

TO PREPARE: Wear closed-toe shoes, pants, and long sleeves. Take a glassblowing class or find an expert to instruct you.

THE WORK:

1. While prepping the oven, meditate on creation—how the very act changes a person and has the power to improve them.

2. When ready to melt the glass, bless the pole by pouring your energies into it, but instead of thinking of them as yours, feel the power as a shard of glass, a small sliver in the greater work that connects everything.

3. As you heat the material, chant, sing, or whisper words honoring the god(s)/universe, elements, and existence through the glass that is to be.

4. When it is time to blow the glass, imagine your breath as the breath of life, as that of the god(s)/universe and eternity.

5. Repeat as needed, then meditate when sealing and transferring glass to the annealing oven. Once removed, chant, sing, or whisper words about the object and its sacred nature.

6. After finishing with the grinding block, stand and hold the glass up to the sky, breathing deep. Set the glass on the floor and stare at it from above. Feel its matter and its importance. Bow to it.

FATED GLASS (FOR FINDING YOUR WAY)

MATERIALS NEEDED: Glass oven/annealing oven, sand/glass, glass pipe, heat resistant gloves, pipe stand, steel tweezers, wood block, grinding block, self

TO PREPARE: Wear close-toed shoes, pants, and long sleeves. Take a glassblowing class or find an expert to instruct you.

THE WORK:

1. Prep the oven and get the materials ready. When it is time to melt, bow to the pole and slide it over the fire.

2. Gaze into the heat. Feel it radiating. Meditate on the unfinished glass and how it moves until finished. See yourself as that material. How are you unfinished? What design do you wish to find yourself made into? How can you get there?

3. When it is time, move the pole onto the stand and blow the glass, but as you do so build your energies. Let each breath build your power internally, but hang on to it. Let the work aid you and carry its electricity inside your chest as you blow.

4. Watch how the glass shapes. Meditate on each change. See yourself in the glass.

5. Study the surface. Chant, sing, or whisper for guidance from the god(s)/universe.

6. Images, words, or ideas will come to you. Direct them toward answering your questions and helping you determine what is best for you.

7. Finish the work and ground yourself. Make use of the knowledge found during this spell.

LOOKING TO THE PAST/FUTURE

MATERIALS NEEDED: Newly finished glasswork, salt, water, sage, five candles (carve four with symbols of the elements), self

TO PREPARE: Create a new piece of glasswork. Perform this spell on the next full moon. Set an altar with four candles at each direction: north, south, east, and west. Put the fifth candle in the middle and place the glass art closest to you on the altar.

THE WORK:

1. Cast a circle with the salt and water, chanting of welcoming the god(s)/ universe and the elements. Light sage and wave it over the glass.

2. Now kneel before the altar and light the elemental candles, calling upon all four powers to aid you individually.

3. Rub your hands on the glass, breathing deeply. Meditate on all the time and effort it took to create it. Reflect on how you tapped into energies used by people of the past and how that aid continues to the future.

4. Light the fifth candle and meditate on how the glass illuminates. Bend down if needed, but get into a comfortable position where the lights dance through the glass. Watch how it flickers and jumps. Look for symbols and images. Breathe in the sage and push your mind to look beyond what is regularly seen.

5. If you are wishing to do so, look back to recall past ancestors, friends, and events. Let them glide through your mind with ease until visions appear. If wishing to look forward, visualize the coming minutes, hours, then days. See the world as it will be in a realistic light and let the glass show you what it will.

6. When exhausted, open the circle and lie back. Ground yourself in the present and ponder what you learned.

CLEAR SUCCESS SPELL

(Prosperity spell)

MATERIALS NEEDED: Newly finished glasswork, salt, water, sage, four candles, each carved with one symbol of the elements), a penny, self

TO PREPARE: Create a new glasswork. Perform this spell on the next new moon. Set an altar with four candles at each end: north, south, east, and west. Put the penny in the middle and place the glass art closest to you on the altar.

THE WORK:

1. Cast a circle with the salt and water, chanting of welcoming the god(s)/universe and the elements. Light sage and wave it over the glass.

2. Stand before the altar and light the candles, welcoming the powers of the elements individually.

3. Take up the penny and rub it between your thumb and forefinger, first with your dominant hand, then the other. Hold it up above your head and sing, chant, or whisper about prosperity and success. Though the penny may not hold much monetary value anymore, it is still a powerful symbol; without it, no further wealth can accrue.

4. Place the penny in the center of the altar and take up the glass. Carefully hold it up. Look through it and visualize yourself achieving business goals, creating useful items others will need or enjoy, and/or following your path toward a positive outcome. Place the glass on the altar once again.

5. Now sing, chant, or whisper words of success and prosperity while dancing around the altar. Let the motion build your energy. Let the power flow through you until you feel ready to burst. Then place your hands on glass and pour that energy into it, focusing on attaining the end you seek.

6. Sit back and open the circle. Rest, ground yourself. Feast if you can, then bow to the altar and your purpose.

Blacksmithing

The practice of forging tools and weapons from metals is thousands of years old. Over three thousand years ago, people were melding and shaping through the practice of blacksmith work. Not many people continue this tradition in modern society. There are plenty of machines and technologies that do much of the dangerous work for everyone. This ancient art has been made obsolete and unnecessary all over industrialized nations, but there are still those who choose to keep the art alive, to carry on the ways of old.

I am lucky enough to be related to a blacksmith (by marriage). As a gift before we were married, my husband helped his cousin forge a gorgeous dagger which we now use in most of our rituals and ceremonies. It is very precious to me as is the practice that allowed it to come into being through the will and hard work of people I know and care about.

Blacksmithing does come with a heavy load. Having researched it to begin my own trials, I have found that it can be harmful to one's health. The proper gear and equipment is necessary to prevent lung issues, burns, and more. Recognizing these hazards and working around them presents the issues people worked to solve in the past and in turn makes the work more valuable. The level of difficulty requires more focus and dedication, a fact itself that creates more drive, more purpose. It heats the fires inside and calls upon higher instincts in need of tending.

Handiwork in the form of forging metals directly encourages deeper thinking, acting, and connecting. When linking actions with thoughts and the connection they bring to life, it is easier to appreciate what is instead of what isn't.

For the smith, the secrets of the earth spill out. A primitive honesty is released through the craft. That honesty holds a simple beauty that still awes people today. Though fewer individuals take up the practice, the work of a good blacksmith is still very much appreciated. Within the work and the metals forged lies the potential to cast spells as strong as the earth from which they are born.

Spells

Because blacksmithing has been around for so long and has been perfected through generations, incorporating spells into the practice is highly potent. Only those who are confident in their forging and hammering abilities should expand their skills with the following spells.

Once you are experienced and fully ready, these few spells host a surge of energy that lasts for years to come.

BLACKSMITHING STRENGTH SPELL

Materials Needed: Forge, anvil, hammers, metal, optional chisels or punches for designing, solid tongs, gloves are also optional

To Prepare: Have design already planned out, all materials ready, and heat up forge. Best done during a waxing moon.

The Work:

1. Start heating the metal in the forge. Flex every muscle as the metal heats up.

2. Meditate on the metal as it begins to glow. Focus on its strength and how it is still the same material when melted to a flexible temperature.

3. Take the piece out and begin hammering. Use the full force of your body. Build your energies with each strike. Let the rhythm of the impact become a drum beat.

4. Shape the metal but as you do so chant, sing, or whisper of the metal's strength. Feel the electricity of the design as you impress your will upon it. Draw that power from the material into your hands, up your arms, and throughout your body.

5. Visualize yourself getting stronger, utilizing that strength for your higher purpose, creating more things.

6. When finished, let the work cool. Step back. Look to the sky and express whatever needs to be released—scream, laugh, sigh. Release all tension to ground the self once more. So mote it be.

METAL FOLDING BINDING

Materials Needed: Forge, anvil, hammers, metal, optional chisels or punches for designing, solid tongs, gloves are also optional

To Prepare: Have design already planned out, all materials ready, and heat up the forge. Best done during the day of a waning moon phase.

The Work:

1. Heat the metal in the forge and begin hammering and folding to shape a sword, dagger, or other sacred work.

2. Meditate on the swing of the blow, the energy coming down upon the metal. Let the energy build inside you.

3. Visualize the issue or the negativity of an individual needing to be bound from harming you. Chant, sing, or whisper about reshaping this imbalance with the power of the elements in the name of the god(s)/universe.

4. Pound the meaning and the problem into the metal. See it change and reform into something better, an aid to protect you.

5. Fold the problem deep inside the material until it is locked away and transformed so well that you feel bonded to it. (Should come around the finishing stage.)

6. Cool the metal then take it up in both hands. Stand outside under the sun. Raise the new creation to the sky. Chant, sing, or whisper to seal the binding under the power of the elements and ask the god(s)/universe to honor your work.

7. Lay the handiwork on the ground in front of you and toss a handful of dirt over it. Kneel down and place hands on it.

8. Meditate on balancing the power forged within the metal. Visualize the object surging with protective energies.

9. Bow to the work and ground the self. It is done.

WEAPON/TOOL BLESSING

Materials Needed: Finished metal work; bucket of blessed water; glass of ale, wine, or water; self

To Prepare: Create your metal work and perform this just after finishing.

The Work:

1. Right after finishing metal work, submerge it in the bucket of blessed water.

2. Stand before it. Breathe deep and close your eyes. Meditate on the energy put into the metal, all the effort pushed into the work.

3. When ready, pull the metal from the water. Raise it up to the sky and chant, sing, or whisper a call to the god(s)/universe asking for a blessing. Dance or sway if compelled to do so.

4. Bow head and kneel. Place both hands on metal and visualize your energy as a glowing light hot enough to influence the strong material. Pour that heat into the object until it warms under your hands.

5. Set the newly crafted item on the ground and get up. Scream, shout, or yell. Take up your drink and toast to the blessing, drink most of the contents, then pour the rest on the metal work.

6. Ground yourself and it is finished.

10
TRUST

When connecting to our instincts, we must learn to trust our purpose, our selves. If we cannot trust our own intuition, we will second-guess the power inside and block our ability to flourish spiritually. The necessity to listen to the inner voice and decipher the difference between needs, wants, and regrets is powerful.

Trusting those voices to understand our needs better encourages those inner parts the courage to speak up when facing the doubt of others. Knowing when to quell desires and when to indulge them becomes another element of trust that builds the character of a truly divine spirit, as does learning how to cope with regret and fully recover from it, using the failed or mistaken experience as a learning tool for a better future.

Meditations, ritual, and spellwork all build trust within, allowing a person to accomplish more for their benefit and the benefit of others. These practices also build power, but only after that trust is strengthened and fine-tuned.

Meditations, rituals, and spellwork help me find the answers I seek, but none of these practices would be successful without trust. Many times, others have questioned me and my abilities. If I had not built enough self-trust to know that I have nothing to prove then I would not be able to continue on my journey of self-awareness and purpose in life.

Once cannot properly interpret their instincts without lending themselves the trust they deserve. There is a meditation that provides the insight one needs to determine what they must do for themselves and how that is obtained. Once achieved, the full connection to nature is born and will breed better connections to others throughout life. It is highly involved and requires a solid block of time:

1. Clear a space to sit and meditate. Gather the fundamental needs of life: a garment, food, and water. Open a window or sit in a space lit by the sun or moon.

2. Sit and place the items around you. The cloth in your lap, the food to your left, water to your right. Let the air and light pour down on you (though it will of course move in time; remain where you are).

3. Close your eyes. Rub your hands over the piece of clothing. Think of its purpose: clothing prevents exposure, protects the body from extreme weather, and sometimes displays your personality.

4. Bow your head. Think of the need to survive and how much that determines what you make, trade, or purchase.

5. Set the cloth in front of you. Now take up the food. Eat a bite. Chew slowly and become conscious of the texture. Absorb the flavor on your tongue. Feel the satisfaction of swallowing and filling your stomach. Think of food's role in your life, how it fuels and nourishes, how it determines your health and your ability to survive.

6. Bow your head. Think of food in terms of nutrition, not taste. Acknowledge that some of the most medicinal meals are not as tantalizing but hold more long-term benefits. Think of how much this determines what you cook and buy.

7. Finish the food and take up the water. Drink a sip. Let the cool hydration surge through your body. Recognize your connection to water. It is not just something to consume but an element that makes up most of your body. It flows through you like a river.

8. Bow your head. Think of refreshing not only your body with the water, but the mind.

9. Now look up. Breathe in. Raise your arms through the invisible air. Let your fingers dance through the light.

10. Slowly bring your hands down to rest on your lap. Refocus yourself. Close your eyes. Visualize these necessities coming together to maintain life, all life and *your* life.

11. See them in your mind. See yourself making use of these necessities. Is there anything missing? What else balances you? Friendship or love?

12. Ties to others that one cannot see or touch remain a determining factor of who we are. They may not keep a person alive, but do keep the spirit thriving. Look past material objects. Instead of seeking instruments, think of singing. Instead of seeking arts, think of expression. Instead of seeking chemicals, think of gaining full trust and control over your being.

13. Explore until exhausted and then ground yourself.

Accomplishments

Invoking the power of truth is an accomplishment in itself. Finding guides and texts that offer unbiased information to offer expansion and progress is a quest that never ends. When meeting a goal or finding another level of thinking a person should celebrate that accomplishment and acknowledge their forward momentum.

Meditating on each new achievement and looking foward to future ones is essential.

1. Sit or lie down in a comfortable space. Stare ahead and think of your most recent accomplishment. No matter how big or small, it deserves your attention. Think of how it came out, the route you took. Are you proud of it? Did you help others along the way? (These are elements that offer balance.)

2. Repeat the first step with each accomplishment of the past few months or even year.

3. Then close your eyes. Clear the mind.

4. Now focus on your latest goal or list of goals. What do you need? What do you want?

5. Now visualize the different paths you may take to obtain this goal. Explore each possibility for success. Which way is more balanced? Which route best fulfills needs and wants and also aids others?

6. Exhaust the possibilities and then open your eyes.

7. Breathe deeply and dedicate yourself to what you know is right and work for it.

Family

Truth in family is not about right or wrong. It has nothing to do with facts coming before or behind feelings. Instead, it is an energy that requires understanding.

It is not always easy for relations to agree or even find harmony and joy together. There will always be disagreements, tiffs, and the occasional feud. How a person handles those struggles is what brings out their honest self. Pushing aside excuses and differences to do what is best for everyone takes a special power that needs tending. It draws out the best of humanity, even though the returns are not immediate.

Family doesn't always have to be blood related. Adopted families and friends bonded so close they become family also hold the same instincts to protect and care for each other. The needs and wants are similar if not identical, and these relationships contain the same elements of love and honesty that everyone needs to find their way to a greater purpose.

When coming together for a family meditation circle or prayer, simplicity is most important. Everyone has their own skill level, a fact that must be respected. The following can be done for immediate kin or at large extended functions.

1. Come together in the same space. Designate an elder to lead.

2. Sit or stand in a circle and hold hands.

3. Have everyone close their eyes and clear their mind.

4. Now chant, sing, or pray together thanking the god(s)/universe for bringing everyone together and for all the gifts of life that bond the family. (The activity can end here, but there is more to be done if participants are willing.)

5. Walk in a circle, chanting/singing/dancing about the circle turning with life and love. Quicken everyone's steps faster and faster until the

elder cannot go any more. Base every movement, stopping and starting, on the leader's actions.

6. Have everyone sit and go around the circle talking about what coming together and being a family means to them.

Community

A sense of community strengthens people's faith in humanity. It connects individuals on a basic level in a space that all parties care for. Building trust with neighbors provides greater protections from intruders and offers a support system in times of tragedy.

I found my voice within the Pagan community. Minority communities give those without as much mainstream support the encouragement they need to be who they are regardless of what they look like, where they come from, who they love, or what kind of pizza toppings they prefer. I myself am an avid fan of pineapple on pizza, but I won't make anyone else eat it if they don't want to, and that is how I view different communities, literal or figurative.

When a town or city of people come together, their energies can be directed toward a common goal that offers healing power after tragedy, strength in times of need, and survival even when death is at everyone's doorstep. No matter which form of community a person supports, involvement is based on a level of interest. The more involved, the more connected a person is and the deeper their energies and greater purpose becomes embedded in the community's common goals.

A community's desires can shift with new generations and/or migration. Some communities want to cling to their ways, others wish to embrace modernity and push changes into being. A healthy mixture is often what appeases all members, because when dealing with a large group of people finding balance and a common ground is more important.

Allowing yourself to be present for your neighbors as much as yourself accomplishes more than you would if you hid inside your home alone. Reaching out to others is also an extension of trust that sparks the magic held within the powers of love and trust themselves. Those forces can be strengthened and put to use for the betterment of everyone.

To bring people together within a community hosting an event like my home town's annual Pagan Picnic is very helpful:

1. Gather everyone together in a circle at a park or large space.

2. Hold hands and breathe deep as one.

3. Have a speaker or multiple people ready to offer some words of wisdom that focus on togetherness.

4. Have everyone raise hands and chant or exhale together.

Nation

A nation is nothing more than a large network of communities. When looking upon it as such, it is easier for a person to better find their fit and seek understanding. Combining energies and swaying powers on a large scale is a task that must serve a broad purpose.

Every nation has its struggles, but when the people come together, they are at their best. Collective efforts and causes bring us all closer over time. And part of coming together as a nation means accepting what has been done, rebuilding, helping those harmed, and finding power in forgiveness and redemption. This is no easy task.

Combined energies charge communities, empower families, and direct individuals down the path that is best for them. Appreciating and trusting in these exercises of national oneness is part of making way for a higher purpose that involves everyone.

Moments of silence, national holidays, and celebrations connect everyone within a nation and draw our energies together.

1. A date must be set and everyone notified publicly.

2. Have everyone stop what they are doing either at work, home, or when out and bow their heads.

3. The energies directed during a moment of silence or during the opening ceremony for a celebration will combine to create an unstoppable force.

Planet

The earth is home. No matter where we go, our feet can always touch it; it never leaves us. Some experience a deeper connection to the planet than others. The wild calls to those who listen. Instincts twitch, readying us to break free and take the lead when we might not have any idea of how to proceed.

If humans wish to continue to be welcomed and nurtured by Mother Nature, we must adhere to the needs of our great home. The earth needs balance. A proper mixture of life and death, and growth and decay is necessary for the planet's survival.

Life is an accomplishment; resilience and survival are accomplishments in the grand scheme of existence. Though imperfect, nature's ability to adapt and change based on what it goes through is a system built to be perfectly imperfect. It does not have to follow one strict set of rules because there are always exceptions. There is always room to shift and change, to improve or birth new species, land masses, and energies.

Celebrations like Earth Day honor this power. For everyone to connect to this great purpose:

1. Unplug as many electronics and devices as possible for Earth Hour or longer.
2. While doing so, focus on healing the planet and honoring it for all its gifts.
3. Afterward, try to be conscious of actions and everyone's responsibility to care for the earth.

Universe

The universe craves movement. It never stops growing or changing. It expands and contracts as if breathing or connecting with all the areas of being.

This motion, this constant network of improvement and newness is akin to humanity's obsession with progress and innovation. They are the same entity. The universe speaks to those who listen because we are part of the universe as much as it is a part of us.

Instead of thinking about life and existence as "real" or "perception," a more accurate representation is energy, fluidity, and ability.

Like everything else, humans host energies. We can build and shape them. That creates a fluid connection to our surroundings and better bonds the spirit beyond the body to outer existences. When properly done, that creates new abilities, new intellectual avenues for the enlightened individual.

Any form of motion appeases the universe because even backward (or destructive) processes can lead toward new branches, new pathways that veer back to the best course. What kills the spark of life and the vibrations of existence is nothingness—emptiness, a statuesque lifestyle and an attitude of not doing anything with oneself.

Spells, meditations, and connection are all great achievements of the universe. They are the communicators that deliver numerous energies to specific powers and keep existences moving. They are great works that feed a higher purpose, that awaken individual meaning while bringing all truths together to form one great work.

To tap into the energies of the universe, meditation needs to look beyond the living and focus more on the energies that connect all of time, everything that has ever been or will be:

1. Sit beneath a starry sky and relax your eyes.

2. Focus on the energies drawing you as an individual toward other people, creatures, and endeavors.

3. Feel that force and hold on to its power. Let it direct your thoughts. Give up control.

Spells

Magic cannot exist without truth. Whether lying to ourselves or others, we cannot find true spiritual growth through falsehoods. Spells do not follow imbalance; they right it.

Personal power begins with being true to one's self so an individual is better able to reach beyond just their own interests and weave their energies with those of the rest of the world and beyond.

Remaining humble enough to understand that one single being cannot possibly know what is right for everyone and everything else while also trusting in fate and how one's own fate is intertwined with that of the whole of creation is a feat not anyone can properly face, yet there are spells that offer aid in that cause.

IMPROVING ONE'S ATTITUDE

How a person sees the world defines much of what they experience. If approaching even the worst of life with the right attitude, anyone can overcome anything.

MATERIALS NEEDED: Blessed salt and water, sage, matches, five white candles (carve four with different element symbols and the fifth one to represent you), mirror, favored stone, shell, or piece of nature

To PREPARE: Set an altar facing north with the element candles at their proper points and the fifth candle in the center. Set the piece of nature on the altar between the candles at the south end. Set salt and water in between the center candle and the east and west sides. Set the mirror between the center and north candle. Best done on a new moon or during waxing period.

THE WORK:

1. Stand before the altar at the south end facing north. Light the sage and walk counterclockwise to cleanse the air. Once back in place wave the sage over the altar completely.

2. Now take up the salt. Sprinkle it in a circle around the altar calling upon the powers of earth, air, fire, and water, with the aid of the god(s)/universe. When all the way around toss a small amount on the mirror and altar.

3. Then take up the water and turn. Sprinkle the water over the salt to seal the circle, walking clockwise now. Chant of sealing the circle by the powers of the elements in the name of the god(s)/universe. When all the way around wet hands and reach up, then bend down to touch the ground.

4. Stand before the candles and light each of the elemental candles, first meditating on representing each one's individual energies and uses. Raise arms to the sky and sing, chant, or shout of your desire to look for better possibilities, to see things for their potential instead of their failures and better direct your energies with balance and grace.

5. Kneel before the candle. Touch it with both hands. Feel your energies build. Let them grow and reach through your body. Send them into the candle.

6. Grab the mirror and hold it over your head. Speak to yourself of seeing everything as it truly is, to look beyond short-term outcomes and extend your energies toward the beauty that may come from destruction, to appreciate the storm for the balance it brings in its fleeting time.

7. Now turn the mirror on the candle. Ask yourself to see life as more than just a reflection of yourself. Know that the instinct of self-preservation may be strong but the instinct to seek fulfillment and happiness is also important.

8. Pick up the candle and place the mirror under it. Now light the candle. Look at yourself from all angles. Love yourself as a whole being who wishes to better themselves and others but without domineering or badgering.

9. Grasp your favorite stone, shell, or other small object from nature. Cover it with both hands. Sit back and meditate on the importance of every piece of nature, existence.

10. Now stand. Place the object on the mirror beside the candle in the center. Walk around the altar. Dance, sing, smile, and laugh. Conjure the best of yourself from the inside out and welcome the god(s)/universe to bless the endeavor.

11. When your energy reaches its peak, turn toward the altar and hold your hands over the candle. Instead of pushing power out, draw it from the candle. Let the heat warm and comfort you in your new endeavor. Take the power in and be at peace with the world.

BLESSING NEW ROUTINES

Materials Needed: Your most used work space at home: desk, kitchen counter, table, etc.; sage; blessed water and salt; wine, ale, or water

To Prepare: Gather materials at the work space in no particular order. Best done on the night of a full moon.

The Work:

1. Stand before the work space. Place both hands on it palms down. Close your eyes and feel the energy of the area.

2. Meditate on yourself and your new routine.

3. Open your eyes and light the sage. Wave it over the area and yourself. Chant, sing, or whisper about new beginnings and how they tie to what remains.

4. Dip your fingers in the salt and rub them over the surface.

5. Now dip your fingers in the water and do the same.

6. Call upon the powers of the elements by the powers of the god(s)/universe.

7. Take up a drink and hold it up in honor of existence and your role in it. Give a toast and drink to the new endeavor. It is done.

FINDING THE GIVER INSIDE

It is easy to get lost in budgets and finances. Bills are aplenty in this day in the modern era, but if a person is not donating any of their income *or* time to their community and the causes they feel are most important than they are not fulfilling the instinct to reach out to others and do something for the betterment of that which they believe in.

MATERIALS NEEDED: A dollar, a piece of paper, a pen

TO PREPARE: Meditate on what needs and wants are being met in your life.

THE WORK:

1. Hold the dollar up to the light. Study it. What kind of energy does it give?

2. Meditate on the answer. Is this single article of money worth all the work we do to earn it? Is it worth our energy, our efforts?

3. Grab the pen and paper. Write down the three most important things that money secures for your lifestyle.

4. Now flip over the paper. On the back, write your three favorite *free* aspects of life, things that do not cost any money.

5. Look back to the other side. Below the list of the three things, write down or draw a picture of all the things you have that cost money. A home? Vehicle? Clothes? Food? Books? Everything. (Write in the margins and all over the paper.)

6. Flip the paper over. Below the free aspects of life you enjoy most, list all the people you know of or have witnessed who are in need and living without the items you have. Think of how it must feel to be them. Would you want pity or understanding? Opportunity or invisibility? Be completely honest.

7. If the first side—the one listing your monetary wealth—holds more writing than the back, meditate on the prospect of donating funds to charity. If the back side holds more writing than the front, meditate on volunteering your time to help others. Even when we are struggling, there is always something to give.

8. Consider the possibility of doing both, and find a realistic balance. Everyone has something to give, whether it is time or funds. Too often it is easy to say, "I don't make enough" or "I'm struggling myself," but that is a foolish mentality that keeps us in a selfish cycle. Giving and offering whatever we can expands the love inside. It brings truth and honor. Breathe deep and accept this responsibility. Live it. Share it.

MENDING RELATIONSHIPS

MATERIALS NEEDED: Long blanket or scarf (long enough to go around people fighting—if needed, tie multiple scarves together), one candle for each person involved, food and drink for a feast

TO PREPARE: Gather family members who are at odds but ready to work through their issues. Also include an elder and others who wish to offer positive energy to the spell.

THE WORK:

1. Stand in a circle. Hold hands and have the elder start a chant or blessing for everyone to say about healing wounds and mending the family.

2. Now have the individuals who are having issues sit in the center, back to back.

3. Hand them each a candle. Have them meditate on the candle pushing out the pain, or frustration held within.

4. Now tie the people together with blanket or scarf while singing, chanting, or whispering words of compromise and understanding.

5. Light the candle of the older person involved in the dispute. Have them bow their head and express what is ailing them in a respectful way without interruption.

6. In the order of age from eldest to youngest (if multiple people are involved), light the next candle and have those individuals do the same until all candles are lit.

7. Have the remaining people circle the two conflicting with arms outspread. Sing a familiar song that connects everyone in the family and let the melody work with everyone's energies, the flames, and cloth.

8. When finished, have elder walk around individuals tied together and kiss each forehead, untie the binds, and have them face each other.

9. There may be no words, or many. Let the spell determine how they proceed to accept what has happened and move on as equals.

10. Have everyone come together in the center and offer their love/hugs. So mote it be.

PASSING WISDOM ON

MATERIALS NEEDED: Elder and youth, objects from important moments in life (e.g., a favorite childhood toy, a letter from a teenage friend, souvenirs from stages of adulthood: before and after having children or raising creatures)

TO PREPARE: Have children expel energy running and playing until they are tired. Then bring them before the elder. Have them sit on the floor before the elder who may stand or sit in a chair.

THE WORK:

1. The elder takes up the first object. Asks children to stare at it and send their best energies to it while telling a story from the past.

2. After the story is told, elder must close their eyes and pour all the energy and love from that memory into the object.

3. The elder will then pass the object to the nearest child and instruct the young ones to be careful, but to hand it around taking a moment each, to examine it and feel the energy warming them and their lives.

4. When brought back to the elder, they will then take a moment to kiss it and then move on to the next object and memory. Repeat the process until finished with all objects.

BONDING YOUNG

MATERIALS NEEDED: A fair-sized rock or gemstone, chisel, hammer, and two or more children

TO PREPARE: Best done on a full moon or waxing moon cycle.

THE WORK:

1. Have the children sit facing each other. If there are more than two, have them make a circle.

2. Place the rock or stone in the middle of them.

3. Have the children stare at the stone and clear their minds.

4. Now have them close their eyes. Advise them to think of the stone as themselves and the warmth that lives within their bodies. Ask them to send that warmth to the rock.

5. Take the chisel and hammer and split the rock into as many pieces as there are children. Try to make the pieces as equal as possible, but educate the children on the fact that the shape and size of their stone will represent them and their connection to the other child(ren). If extras break off, give to the parents afterward.

6. Hand the pieces out accordingly.

7. Give the children a few moments to hold and look over their stones.

8. Now have them set it down in their place and stand up. Tell them to step back and make a larger circle.

9. Instruct them to walk in a circle, slowly at first but then speeding up to seal the rite. Allow them to dance and sing, skip, or leap about and run as they choose.

10. When they are exhausted, have them stop before their stone and pick it up. Ask them to feel its energy and hold it up to the sky.

11. Now lead them in a chant/song to bless their connection to each other.

12. Have everyone bow and take their stones. Let them know that they need to look after it. (If willing, make the stones/gems into a piece of jewelry for them to wear.)

FINDING WHAT IS BEST IN A DIVIDED SITUATION

MATERIALS NEEDED: Staff or large stick, handful of dirt (from the area) for everyone, space with surrounding greenery, community leader(s), group of people within the community

To PREPARE: Research all sides of the issue. Try to find as many unbiased opposing facts as possible to be ready for whatever comes. This practice is best for new developments and issues that are being debated but have not yet come to pass.

THE WORK:

1. Come together in public area that is well-known to the community. Place the dirt in the center of the circle. Sit or stand in a circle.

2. Have the leader(s) hold the staff and have their say. Then pass the staff around to each person present giving them their time to voice their concerns and wishes.

3. Now bring everyone to the center to grab a small handful of dirt.

4. Reform the circle and have everyone hold up their dirt. The leader(s) must now speak some words of togetherness and finding their way through the issue together.

5. Then disperse and have everyone gently place their dirt along the greenery together.

6. Come back to the area where the circle was formed and once more discuss solutions with the leader(s) and find a common ground.

BLESSING POSITIVE TRADITIONS

MATERIALS NEEDED: Community group, elder(s) or leader(s), black and white ribbons for everyone

To PREPARE: Prepare the ribbons with a pin or braid into bracelets or necklaces for wearing.

THE WORK:

1. Before a community tradition/recurring event, the elder(s)/leader(s) must place their hands over the ribbons and push energies of connectedness into them.

2. Place the ribbons in plain view at the event so they can absorb the atmosphere.

3. At the end of a community traditional/recurring event, bring everyone together.

4. The elder(s)/leader(s) should speak, sing, or chant of their strength, how together they bond their lives to those sharing their community and how positive that is.

5. Instruct everyone to line up and receive their ribbons from the elder(s)/leader(s) one by one.

FORMING A BETTER WAY

MATERIALS NEEDED: A candle for everyone, staff or large sick, elder(s)/leader(s), as many community members as possible

TO PREPARE: Best done directly after tragedy strikes.

THE WORK:

1. The designated elder/leader must set a time and place, then meet everyone accordingly holding the staff.

2. They will then chant, sing, or speak words of how the pain has hit the community and what is needed to move forward while holding the staff out to draw in everyone's power. Pull it in and use it.

3. Have the elder go around to light everyone's candles one at a time. The energies build better when the light comes from the same source which in this case is the designated elder/leader person.

4. Let the light shine. Let the heat build. Feel the energies mingle in the aftermath. But this does not seal the rite; everyone must remain until the candles burn out. Everyone must see the pain and the beauty in their community members.

5. Once the candles have burned out, the elder/leader should hold up the staff and slam the end to the ground. The energies drawn in at the beginning of this spell will be ready to go back out. And when compelled by the god(s)/the universe, the designated elder/leader will then know what to say and how to leave everyone with hope for the future.

HONORING THE FALLEN

MATERIALS NEEDED: The will of the people, silence

To PREPARE: The president/leader or some other official will designate a moment of silence. This common practice is the seed for a spell if enough members of the Pagan community combine forces to sway the energies surrounding the action.

THE WORK:

1. Go outside just before the designated moment of silence.

2. Reach up and expand your personal energies. Bend forward and reach down to grasp for the ground.

3. Chant, sing, or whisper, asking the gods/universe to honor the coming silence. Feel the element prepare for it.

4. Close your eyes. When it is time, fall silent but let your power build and grow. Send it out of your body in a healing light. Visualize it expanding through your home, community, and across the nation.

5. Give in to the feeling and do not fear any out-of-body experiences that may follow.

6. When exhausted, open your eyes and ground yourself. Balance your energies and go feast and toast to the fallen.

STRENGTHENING THE PEOPLE

MATERIALS NEEDED: The will of the people, a balanced mind, wine or water for everyone with you in attendance, communications devices (optional)

To PREPARE: Meditate beforehand, working to center yourself no matter where your politics reside to better connect with everyone, especially those who hold opposing viewpoints. Come together with others during an inauguration, important speech, or another important national event.

THE WORK:

1. Stand with the group during the event.

2. Have everyone take up a glass of wine or water.

3. Watch, listen to, or think of the event. Be perceptive and respectful. Respect extended to those we agree with is not a challenge to our minds or greater purpose. To offer respect to those we disagree with even when they do not offer it to us allows a pure and truthful purpose for our workings and charges the rite with more energy.

4. While doing so, have everyone involved meditate on extending their energies to the betterment of all people.

5. At the end of the event, have everyone raise up their glasses. Chant, sing, or shout words together, words of unity and being strong as a people.

6. Feast and celebrate the freedoms and joys that exist or are hoped to exist.

BALANCING PRIDE AND HUMILITY

MATERIALS NEEDED: The will of the people, a balanced mind, money and/or food (to donate)

TO PREPARE: Do during a big public national celebration such as New Year's Eve or the Fourth of July. Get other Pagans organized to go with or do on their own simultaneously.

THE WORK:

1. Go to parade or celebration with the money or food in your pocket or on your person. Be a part of the crowd. Let go and celebrate without judging others.

2. During the height of the excitement, meditate on your energies. Build them, grow them, and extend the power beyond your body. Send it out into the area and beyond.

3. Step back and hold the money or food and visualize it helping/nourishing others.

4. Find a nearby charity (many participate in events) or seek out someone who looks like they are in need. Go and give them your offering. (Charities cannot take food unless collecting nonperishables—keep this in mind.) Be smart, trust your instincts, but do not fear giving to others. Push away all thought of your own struggles. Just focus on balancing the energy of celebration with the act of giving to others so they have more cause to celebrate.

EARTH DAY BLESSING

MATERIALS NEEDED: Large group of people, and friendly pets

TO PREPARE: Coordinate an event or attend one in honor of Earth Day to celebrate the great planet that supports us all. Try to commit to turning off all electronics and devices. If possible, walk to the event and do not use any artificial energy for the preceding twenty-four hour period.

THE WORK:

1. Come together in a circle. Have pets sit to the left of owners, children to the right of parents.

2. Raise arms up and sing, chant, or shout of coming together for a purpose. For example: "We come together to…"

3. Lower your arms down and sing, chant, or shout that purpose. For example: "Share the earth for all of us."

4. Repeat the above seven times.

5. Have everyone bow their heads for a moment of silence to meditate; visualize a clean, healthy planet; and send that energy out into the world.

6. To seal the rite collect trash and dispose of properly. Then plant trees, shrubs, and/or flowers together.

Specifically casting a spell for trusting the universe itself is the most difficult feat a practitioner will ever face. There is only one spell that will be published here for the universe. Because something so important and beyond human comprehension is beyond full understanding, a single spell to protect existence and its motion is all one can do, which should be done with the utmost care and concentration.

UNIVERSE PROTECTION SPELL

MATERIALS NEEDED: Large group of Pagans or people in tune with their energies, starry night, bonfire, wine or water, blessed salt, body of water, and wildflower seeds

TO PREPARE: Gather a large group on a piece of land near a body of water on a starry night, preferably in summer. Build a bonfire close to the water but far enough away to allow for a circle to be formed around it.

THE WORK:

1. Swim in the natural body of water and meditate on the energies shared while swimming.

2. Leave the water and light the fire. Let the heat and light dry you off, no towels.

3. Pass around a bowl of salt and have each person scatter a handful behind them to craft a circle. Chant or sing together of earth, air, fire, water, and humanity coming together to represent the universe.

4. Then pass around wine or water for everyone to drink together. Toast to the god(s) and or the universe and its encompassing ways.

5. Move counterclockwise together, dancing and clapping with the energy of movement and existence. Visualize eternity and the powers that swirl through everything as you move faster and faster until people begin to lose their balance. Some may feel silly or fall over laughing; tend to whomever needs it. Anyone unable to move with the circle should be placed inside it to clap or chant as they need regardless of level of ability or health.

6. Now stop and hold arms up to the sky, watching the stars glitter overhead. Feel their glow. Embrace their burning motion, the power in that energy.

7. Chant or sing of protecting the great light and darkness that is existence.

8. Then take up a handful of wildflower seeds and plant them in a designated space by the water.

9. Bow to the water and smile at the sky.

CONCLUSION

We are on the verge of a better way. Being part of the shift and solving our current problems is not about being right and furthering political divides—it is about coming together to love and respect every aspect of life. There are many ways to find fulfillment in existence. Connecting with nature to draw out the instincts hidden within us offers humanity the balance needed to live with a higher purpose.

Gardening, hiking, swimming, and tree climbing are all actions that have the potential to remind us of who we are and where we come from, and even just opening a window or tending houseplants reestablishes that bond. These activities enrich our souls.

Meditations, handiwork, and spellwork strengthen the connections between our actions and our more spiritual selves, which increases understanding, intuition, and instinctual ties that link everyone to the universe. Those bonds cultivate trust and lead to the doorway of love.

Love is the most powerful motion of the spirit. The energies and vibrations love inspires and fuels provide more momentum than any other action known to humanity.

The instinct to trust and thrive lives in everyone. It is drawn out by nature and survival. It is the better part of existence. It drives the universe to continue on its journey and does not begin and end with humanity, but all creatures.

To Write to the Author

If you wish to contact the author or would like more information about this book, please write to the author in care of Llewellyn Worldwide Ltd. and we will forward your request. Both the author and publisher appreciate hearing from you and learning of your enjoyment of this book and how it has helped you. Llewellyn Worldwide Ltd. cannot guarantee that every letter written to the author can be answered, but all will be forwarded. Please write to:

Jessica Marie Baumgartner
℅ Llewellyn Worldwide
2143 Wooddale Drive
Woodbury, MN 55125-2989
Please enclose a self-addressed stamped envelope for reply,
or $1.00 to cover costs. If outside the U.S.A., enclose
an international postal reply coupon.

Many of Llewellyn's authors have websites with additional information and resources. For more information, please visit our website at http://www.llewellyn.com.